Especially For Him

by
Hal Burbach

The
AMERICAN
★ COOKING ★
GUILD

Acknowledgements

I would like to extend a special word of apprecia-
tion to Bill Cates for his invaluable contribution to
the publication of this book. Not only has he attend-
ed to every phase of its publication in a highly pro-
fessional manner, he has done it with a combination
of humor, honesty and an uncommon sense of
decency in dealing with other people. he has made
what I have heard others describe as a dreary experience into a very pleasant, growth-oriented one
for me and I am most grateful.

Also, I want to thank my two typists; Ginny Alley
for her work on the earlier drafts and Janet Armour
for promptly turning out the final product.

Cover photograph by John Burwell

Interior art by Jim Haynes

First Printing, October 1982
Second Printing, December 1982
Third Printing, November 1983
Fourth Printing, August 1984
Fifty Printing, November 1984
Sixth Printing, March 1985
Seventh Printing, April 1986

Library of Congress #82050937
ISBN 0-942320-07-7

Published by:
The American Cooking Guild
2915 Fenimore Road
P.O. Box 2691
Silver Spring, Maryland 20902

Table of Contents

Dedication

For my mother, Helen Gillespie Burbach, whose indominable spirit has been a guiding force in my life . . . and for Christy whose unswerving belief in this project together with her love and support have helped me see it through to completion.

INTRODUCTION

Until a few years ago I had never lifted a finger to cook. Somewhere in the aftermath of marital separation, however, I decided to teach myself enough about cooking to at least prepare my own meals. Like most beginners I gravitated toward a trial and error procedure of cooking; I would simply search out a recipe I felt I could do, follow its directions to the letter, and take my chances. Though generally workable, I soon discovered that this approach contained the seeds of two basic types of problems: one, I had to spend what I considered to be an inordinate amount of time paging through cookbooks and magazines looking for doable recipes; and two, I was constantly trying to decipher directions, puzzling over various cooking terms, and looking through my scant collection of cookbooks for information on how to perform one cooking technique (e.g., how to scald milk) or another. At first I interpreted this as "my" problem, but as time wore on and I began to discuss the subject with more and more men, I discovered that they were experiencing the same kinds of difficulties. It was at this point that I sensed the need for a cookbook designed especially for men and it was shortly thereafter that I decided to trade on my first-hand experience in an effort to produce a book aimed at helping the beginner ease his way into the kitchen.

That there is a growing number of men in this country who are becoming interested in learning to cook can hardly be debated. This emerging group is comprised mainly of the more than seven million adult males who now live alone and the inestimably millions more who are sharing their lives with women who feel that men should pull their own weight in the kitchen. Furthermore, the combined effects of a steadily expanding divorce rate, the trend for males to marry at a later age, and the realignment of traditional sex roles in our society are swelling their ranks daily.

This book seeks to anticipate and speak to some of what we are only now beginning to learn about the unique and frequently subtle cooking-related needs of these men. Following, for the reader's quick perusal, is a listing of those which constitute the guiding force behind this work.

1. Perhaps more than anything else, men are needful of a cookbook they can readily comprehend. While the experts who author cookbooks—even beginner's manuals—assume they are writing at a level which virtually any reader can understand, the collective experiences of the men I talked with suggest otherwise. Indeed, nearly all of them gave repeated emphasis to the fact that they often encountered cooking-related terms (clarified butter, pastry blender and colander are a few that come to mind) which eluded their working vocabulary. In addition, most reported that they were frequently frustrated by the jargon, abbreviations, and in-house shorthand that characterize most cookbooks. This is in no way meant to slight or malign existing cookbooks. Rather, it is to suggest that when seen from the vantage point of men who are just beginning to find their way around the kitchen, there is a need for a cookbook that dares to be simple.

2. Men also stand in need of a cookbook that is comprised of recipes that call for procedures and techniques that are within their limited range of abilities. The problem here begins with the simple recognition that while the preponderance of women have spent their formative years being socialized to a female role that has provided them with an impressive array of baseline kitchen skills, the socialization experiences of most men have left them almost totally ignorant in the ways of the kitchen. Of itself, this is no revelation. However, when one considers that cookbooks are written almost exclusively with women and/or experienced men in mind and that as a consequence it is their projected skill level that becomes the lowest common denominator in developing and communicating recipes, the problem comes into sharper focus. Unadorned, it is that inexperienced men are placed at a distinct disadvantage when it comes to finding recipes that they can easily execute and hence they have need of a collection of recipes which is designed to accommodate their meager incoming skills.

3. Still another area of need derives from the fact that many men, particularly those starting over, often do not have the cooking utensils and equipment to execute the full complement of recipes in most cookbooks. In some cases this amounts to little more than a marginal inconvenience, while in others it places a serious limitation on the number of doable recipes in a given book. But in either instance it is a very real problem that can be easily remedied by offering men a grouping of recipes that can be done with a minimum (and I do mean minimum) of apparatus.

4. Whether by choice or circumstance, a sizable portion of men who want to learn to cook will be "going it alone" and for this reason will need all the auxiliary help they can get from a cookbook. While anyone who is willing to spend some time scouting around bookstores could put together a resource library upon which to draw as the need arose, most men simply aren't going to invest the appreciable amount of time, energy and dollars such a course of action would require. This, then, translates into a need for a cookbook that anticipates and brings together in a single volume the sort of background assistance that can make the life of a beginner a self-sufficient one.

More specifically, as every novice is sure to encounter a continual string of terms with which he is unfamiliar, he has a need for a cookbook that contains a glossary. Additionlly, in those not so rare instances in which men find themselves with no kitchen equipment whatsoever, we have nothing if not a built-in need for information on how to stock and equip a kitchen. And whereas men have had little or no experience in menu planning, most could use a little coaching in this important area of the total cooking enterprise. Further, as many men will be interested in learning to cook across a variety of situations, they need ready access to a unitary assortment of recipes that run the gamut from appetizers to desserts, from breakfast to dinner.

What men could use, in sum, is a self-contained cooking guide that will allow those who stand ready to help themselves to solo their way to a base level of cooking competence. And this is precisely what **Especially For Him** is about.

Recipes for Beginners

HOW TO DO A RECIPE

As can be observed from the following example, it's as easy as 1, 2, 3!

— Sample Recipe —

Drop Biscuits

Difficulty rating: VERY EASY   **Serves:** Makes 12-14 biscuits

Equipment needed: Baking sheet   **Estimated preparation time:**
& bowl   20-25 minutes

First:
Scan these sections to determine what you need to execute the recipe.

INGREDIENTS

2   cups all-purpose flour
1   tablespoon baking powder
½   teaspoon salt

⅓   cup shortening
1   cup milk

BASIC STEPS

1. Preheat oven at 450°.

2. In a bowl, combine 2 cups all-purpose flour with 1 tablespoon baking powder and ½ teaspoon salt.

3. Work in ⅓ cup shortening and add 1 cup milk. Mix well.

4. Drop batter by the teaspoon onto an ungreased baking sheet.

5. Bake about 15-20 minutes.

Second:
Follow these step-by-step instructions through to completion.

Third:
Take a few minutes to jot down your suggestions for next time.

Notes:

Appetizers

Cream Cheese and Caviar

Difficulty rating: VERY EASY

Equipment needed: Mixing bowl

Serves: 6-8

Estimated preparation time:
5-10 minutes

INGREDIENTS

1 package (8 ounces) cream
  cheese
½ cup sour cream
1 tablespoon lemon juice

1 jar (4 ounces) red caviar

melba toast

BASIC STEPS

1. In a bowl, combine 1 package (8 ounces) cream cheese, ½ cup sour cream and 1 tablespoon lemon juice.

2. Open 1 jar (4 ounces) red caviar and remove 1 tablespoon to be used later as a garnish.

3. Mix the remaining caviar into the cream cheese and refrigerate.

4. When ready to serve, place the caviar and cream cheese mixture in a serving bowl and garnish with 1 tablespoon red caviar. Serve with melba toast.

Notes:

Prosciutto and Melon

Difficulty rating: VERY EASY

Equipment needed: None

Serves: 3-4

Estimated preparation time:
10 minutes

INGREDIENTS

1 honeydew or cantelope melon

6-8 pieces prosciutto

3-4 lemon wedges

BASIC STEPS

1. Cut 1 honeydew or cantelope melon in half. Remove seeds and cut the melon into elongated sections about 2 inches wide. Remove the rind so only the fruit remains.

2. Wrap each piece of melon with a piece of prosciutto.

3. Divide into desired number of portions and serve on a plate with a wedge of lemon.

Notes:

Hot Crabmeat Dip

Difficulty rating: VERY EASY

Equipment needed: Casserole dish & mixing bowl

Serves: Variable

Estimated preparation time: 40-45 minutes

INGREDIENTS

1 package (8 ounces) cream cheese
2 tablespoons half & half cream
1 can (6 ounces) crabmeat
1 tablespoon horseradish
1 tablespoon Worcestershire sauce
salt and pepper

slivered almonds

assorted crackers

BASIC STEPS

1. In a mixing bowl, blend together 1 package (8 ounces) cream cheese, 2 tablespoons half & half cream, 1 can (6 ounces) crabmeat, 1 tablespoon horseradish and 1 tablespoon Worcestershire sauce. Salt and pepper to taste.

2. Transfer to lightly greased casserole dish and top with slivered almonds and bake at 375° for 30 minutes.

3. Serve hot (in a chafing dish if you have one) with assorted crackers.

Notes:

Baked Brie Wheel

Difficulty rating: VERY EASY

Serves: 5-6

Equipment needed: Baking dish

Estimated preparation time:
20-25 minutes

INGREDIENTS	BASIC STEPS
	1. Preheat oven to 325°.
1 8-ounce Brie wheel	2. Place an 8-ounce Brie wheel in a baking dish.
2 tablespoons butter ¼ cup sliced almonds	3. Dot the Brie with 2 tablespoons butter and cover this with ¼ cup sliced almonds.
	4. Bake about 15 minutes or until heated through.
French bread	5. Serve warm with French bread.

Notes:

Party Cheese Ball

Difficulty rating: VERY EASY

Equipment needed: Mixing bowl

Serves: 6-8

Estimated preparation time:
10-15 minutes

INGREDIENTS

1 tablespoon finely chopped onions
1 tablespoon chopped green olives

1 package (8 ounces) cream cheese
1 package (1½ ounces) Roquefort cheese
1 teaspoon Worcestershire sauce

½ cup English walnuts
2 tablespoons chopped parsely

assorted crackers

BASIC STEPS

1. Finely chop 1 tablespoon onion and 1 tablespoon green olives.

2. In a mixing bowl, blend together 1 package (8 ounces) cream cheese, 1 package (1½ ounces) Roquefort cheese and 1 teaspoon Worcestershire sauce with the onions and green olives.

3. Refrigerate the cheese mixture overnight.

4. Chop ½ cup English walnuts and mix with 2 tablespoons chopped parsely.

5. Shape the cheese into a ball and roll in the nut and parsely mixture.

6. Serve with assorted crackers.

Notes:

Clam Dip

Difficulty rating: VERY EASY

Equipment needed: Mixing bowl

Serves: Variable

Estimated preparation time:
15-20 minutes

INGREDIENTS

1 tablespoon onion

1 package (8 ounces) cream
  cheese
½ cup sour cream
1 can (6 ounces) minced clams
1 teaspoon lemon juice
1 teaspoon Worchestershire
  sauce
  dash of Tabasco sauce
  salt and pepper

crackers and potato chips

BASIC STEPS

1. Finely chop 1 tablespoon onion.

2. In a bowl, blend together 1
package (8 ounces) cream
cheese, ½ cup sour cream, 1 can
(6 ounces) minced clams, 1
teaspoon lemon juice, 1 teaspoon
Worcestershire sauce, the
chopped onions and a dash of
Tabasco sauce. Salt and pepper
to taste.

3. Chill and serve with crackers and
potato chips.

Notes:

Pineapple Cheese Ball

Difficulty rating: VERY EASY

Equipment needed: 2 mixing bowls

Serves: Variable

Estimated preparation time: 15-20 minutes

INGREDIENTS

1½ cups chopped pecans
½ cup fresh chopped parsely

2 packages (8 ounces each) cream cheese
1 can (8 ounces) crushed pineapple

assorted crackers

BASIC STEPS

1. Chop 1½ cups pecans and ½ cup fresh parsely.

2. In a bowl, combine 2 packages (8 ounces each) cream cheese, 1 can (8 ounces) crushed pineapple (drain well) and 1 cup chopped pecans. Shape into a ball.

3. In a separate bowl, toss together ½ cup chopped pecans and ½ cup fresh parsely.

4. Roll the cheese ball in the pecan and parsely mixture until surface in evenly coated.

5. Serve with assorted crackers.

Notes:

Kitchen Tips✔
An excellent way to "chop" fresh parsley is to "snip" it with a pair of scissors.

Cheese Spread

Difficulty rating: VERY EASY

Equipment needed: Mixing bowl & grater

Serves: Variable

Estimated preparation time: 10-15 minutes

INGREDIENTS

½   pound cheddar cheese
¼   pound blue cheese

¼   pound cream cheese
½   pound butter
2   teaspoons Worcestershire sauce
⅛   teaspoon Tabasco sauce

assorted crackers

BASIC STEPS

1. Shred ½ pound cheddar cheese and crumble ¼ pound blue cheese.

2. In a large mixing bowl, blend together the cheddar and blue cheeses with ¼ pound cream cheese, ½ pound softened butter, 2 teaspoons Worcestershire sauce and ⅛ teaspoon Tabasco sauce. Cover and put in refrigerator to chill.

3. Serve in a small bowl or on a plate with assorted crackers.

Notes:

Kitchen Tips
Before grating cheese brush the grater with a little vegetable oil. This will make it easier to wash the cheese off the grater.

Hot Cheese Appetizers

Difficulty rating: VERY EASY

Equipment needed: Baking sheet & mixing bowl

Serves: Variable

Estimated preparation time: 20-30 minutes

INGREDIENTS

¼ cup butter
1 jar (6 ounces) sharp cheese

½ cup all-purpose flour
   dash of Tabasco sauce

BASIC STEPS

1. Soften ¼ cup butter and 1 jar (6 ounces) sharp cheese (set near a gentle heat source such as a radiator or register).

2. In a bowl, combine the softened butter and cheese with ½ cup all-purpose flour and a dash of Tabasco sauce.

3. Refrigerate for 2-3 hours. When ready to serve roll the cheese dough into spheres about the size of ping pong balls.

4. Place on a greased baking sheet and bake in a preheated oven at 350° for 8-10 minutes.

5. Serve warm.

Notes:

Hot Sausage and Cheese Balls

Difficulty rating: VERY EASY

Equipment needed: Skillet, mixing bowl, baking sheet & grater

Serves: Yields 60-70 balls

Estimated preparation time: 40-50 minutes

INGREDIENTS

1 pound ground hot sausage

3 cups all-purpose flour
¾ cup butter or margarine

1 pound grated sharp cheddar cheese

2-4 tablespoons milk

BASIC STEPS

1. Preheat oven at 400°.

2. In a skillet, saute 1 pound ground hot sausage. Drain well and let cool.

3. In a separate bowl, combine 3 cups all-purpose flour and ¾ cup softened butter or margarine.

4. Grate 1 pound sharp cheddar cheese and blend together the sausage. flour and cheese. Add milk, a tablespoon at a time, until mixture gathers into a ball.

5. Shape into spheres about the size of ping pong balls and arrange on a baking sheet. Bake for 15-20 minutes, until nicely browned.

6. Serve warm.

Notes:

Curried Tomato Juice

Difficulty rating: VERY EASY

Equipment needed: Blender

Serves: 5-6

Estimated preparation time: 5-10 minutes

INGREDIENTS

1 quart tomato juice
2 tablespoons lemon juice
2 teaspoons curry powder

celery sticks

BASIC STEPS

1. In a blender, mix together 1 quart tomato juice, 2 tablespoons lemon juice and 2 teaspoons curry powder.

2. Chill and serve with a stick of celery.

Notes:

Kitchen Tips ✓
Place a small bowl of baking soda in your refrigerator. This will keep it fresh smelling and free of offensive odors.

Stuffed Figs

Difficulty rating: VERY EASY

Equipment needed: Mixing bowl

Serves: Yields 2 dozen figs

Estimated preparation time: 10-15 minutes

INGREDIENTS

1 package (8 ounces) cream cheese
2 tablespoons whipping cream

2 dozen figs

BASIC STEPS

1. In a bowl, blend together 1 package (8 ounces) cream cheese and 2 tablespoons whipping cream.

2. Cut a slit in the side of 2 dozen figs and stuff with the cream cheese mixture.

3. Chill before serving.

Notes:

Kitchen Tips ✓
If you have limited counter space, leave out only your everyday appliances (e.g., coffee maker, can opener, etc.) and keep the others in cabinets.

Pepper Slices With Cream Cheese

Difficulty rating: VERY EASY

Equipment needed: Mixing bowl

Serves: 3-4

Estimated preparation time:
5-10 minutes

INGREDIENTS

½ cup ricotta cheese
¼ cup cream cheese
1-2 teaspoons chives

1 green pepper

paprika

BASIC STEPS

1. In a bowl, blend together ½ cup ricotta cheese, ¼ cup cream cheese and 1-2 teaspoons chives.

2. Hollow out 1 green pepper such that it will look like a cup.

3. Stuff the pepper with the cheese mixture and refrigerate overnight.

4. When ready to serve cut pepper into thick slices and sprinkle with paprika.

Notes:

Kitchen Tips ✓
Keep your sharp knives in a separate knife rack and *not* in the drawer with other utensils.

Celery Stuffed With Cream Cheese

Difficulty rating: VERY EASY

Equipment needed: None

Serves: makes about 8-10 ribs of celery

Estimated preparation time: 5-10 minutes

INGREDIENTS

8-10 ribs of celery

1 package (3 ounces) cream cheese

paprika

BASIC STEPS

1. Wash and dry 8-10 ribs of celery (use only narrow and tender ribs).

2. Open 1 package (3 ounces) cream cheese and fill the hollowed part of each rib with the cheese. Leave about 1½ inches at the end of the rib.

3. Sprinkle lightly with paprika and refrigerate until ready to use.

Notes:

Kitchen Tips ✓
The best place for your chopping block is next to the sink. Situated here, it will cut down on mess and save you valuable time.

Grilled Oyster and Bacon Appetizers

Difficulty rating: VERY EASY

Equipment needed: Shallow three-quart baking dish

Serves: Variable

Estimated preparation time: 15-20 minutes

INGREDIENTS	BASIC STEPS
bacon	1. Cut several bacon strips in half.
1 pint oysters lemon salt	2. Spread 1 pint of oysters over the bottom of a shallow baking dish and sprinkle with lemon salt.
	3. Wrap each oyster with a half slice of bacon and fasten with a toothpick.
	4. Place under a broiler until bacon gets crisp (about 3-4 minutes on a side).
lemon wedges	5. Serve with lemon wedges.

Notes:

Kitchen Tips✓

Keep your leftovers on a refrigerator shelf that has been specifically designated for this purpose. This will help keep them from becoming "lost" and in consequence cut down on the amount of food you end up throwing out.

Broiled Scallops Wrapped In Bacon

Difficulty rating: VERY EASY

Equipment needed: Shallow three-quart baking dish

Serves: 4

Estimated preparation time: 20-25 minutes

INGREDIENTS

24-30 scallops
   2 tablespoons lemon juice
    salt and pepper

12-15 strips bacon

   4 wedges lemon
   1 jar tartar sauce

BASIC STEPS

1. Arrange 24-30 scallops on a shallow baking dish. Sprinkle with lemon juice. Salt and pepper to taste.

2. Cut 12-15 strips of bacon in half and wrap 1 piece of bacon around each scallop and secure with a toothpick.

3. Place under a broiler and grill for 5-6 minutes on each side.

4. Serve hot with a wedge of lemon and tartar sauce.

Notes:

Chicken Liver Paté

Dificulty rating: EASY

Equipment needed: Skillet, blender & mixing bowl

Serves: Variable

Estimated preparation time: 20-30 minutes

INGREDIENTS

1 onion
1 clove of garlic
1 cup fresh mushrooms

2-3 tablespoons butter of margarine
2 pounds chicken livers

1 teaspoon lemon juice
1 teaspoon curry powder
1 teaspoon paprika
¼ teaspoon salt
⅛ teaspoon pepper

1 cup butter
¼ cup cognac

assorted crackers

BASIC STEPS

1. Chop 1 onion and 1 clove of garlic. Also, slice 1 cup fresh mushrooms.

2. Heat 2-3 tablespoons butter or margarine in a large skillet and saute 2 pounds chicken livers together with the garlic and onions 8-10 minutes. Add in mushrooms and cook another 3-5 minutes. Drain.

3. In a blender, combine the skillet ingredients with 1 teaspoon lemon juice, 1 teaspoon curry powder, 1 teaspoon paprika, ¼ teaspoon salt and ⅛ teaspoon pepper. Mix throughly.

4. Pour blender ingredients in a large bowl and add in 1 cup butter and ¼ cup cognac. Mix until a uniform consistency is reached.

5. Chill and serve with assorted crackers.

Notes:

Breakfast
Entrees

Health Drink

Difficulty rating: VERY EASY

Equipment needed: Blender

Serves: 1

Estimated preparation time:
5 minutes

INGREDIENTS

- 1 cup skim milk
- 2 tablespoons soya powder
- 1 tablespoon lecithin
- 1 tablespoon wheat germ
- 2 tablespoons brewer's yeast
- 1 tablespoon honey
  cinnamon
  * nutmeg

BASIC STEPS

1. In a blender, combine 1 cup skim milk, 2 tablespoons soya powder, 1 tablespoon lecithin, 1 tablespoon wheat germ, 2 tablespoons brewer's yeast and 1 tablespoon honey. Add a dash of cinnamon and nutmeg and mix for 20-30 seconds.

2. Pour into a glass and set in freezer for 1-2 hours if you have time. If not, drink as is.

3. Retrieve drink from freezer and mix in blender once again for a few seconds. Drink will now have the consistency of a milk shake.

Notes:

Tomato-Protein Drink

Difficulty rating: VERY EASY

Serves: 1

Equipment needed: Blender

Estimated preparation time:
5 minutes

INGREDIENTS

1 cup tomato juice
1 egg
2 tablespoons wheat germ

celery stick

BASIC STEPS

1. In a blender, combine 1 cup tomato juice, 1 egg and 2 tablespoons wheat germ. Mix for 20-30 seconds.

2. Serve with a celery stick.

Notes:

High Protein Orange Drink

Difficulty rating: VERY EASY

Equipment needed: Blender

Serves: 1

Estimated preparation time:
3-5 minutes

INGREDIENTS

1½ cups orange juice
1 egg
1 tablespoon wheat germ

Note: Pineapple or grapefruit juice can be substituted for orange juice.

BASIC STEPS

1. In a blender, mix together 1½ cups orange juice, 1 egg and 1 tablespoon wheat germ.

2. Pour into a juice glass and serve.

Notes:

Kitchen Tips ✓
For richer iced coffee or tea use ice cubes made from same.

Orange Or Pineapple Eggnog

Difficulty rating: VERY EASY

Equipment needed: Blender

Serves: 1

Estimated preparation time:
5 minutes

INGREDIENTS

1 cup milk
1 egg
1 tablespoon honey
½ cup orange or pineapple juice

cinnamon

BASIC STEPS

1. In a blender, combine 1 cup milk, 1 egg, 1 tablespoon honey and ½ cup orange or pineapple juice. Mix for 20-30 seconds.

2. Serve with a sprinkling of cinnamon.

Notes:

Scrambled Eggs

Difficulty rating: VERY EASY

Equipment needed: Skillet & mixing bowl

Serves: Variable—2-3 eggs per person

Estimated preparation time: 5-10 minutes

INGREDIENTS

2-3 eggs per person
  1 tablespoon milk per 2 eggs
    salt and pepper

  1 tablespoon margarine or
    butter

BASIC STEPS

1. Break desired number of eggs into a bowl and add 1 tablespoon of milk per every 2 eggs. Salt and pepper to taste. Mix well with a fork.

2. Heat 1 tablespoon margarine or butter in a skillet using medium-hot heat.

3. Pour eggs into skillet.

4. Scramble them with a fork to desired consistency.

5. Serve immediately.

Note: Eggs continue to cook after you remove them from heat so be careful not to overcook.

Notes:

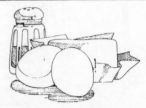

Kitchen Tips ✔
Eggs can "pick up" odors from other foods stored in your refrigerator. Hence, it is a good idea to keep eggs in their original container or cover them in some other appropriate way.

Cottage Cheese Scramble

Difficulty rating: VERY EASY

Equipment needed: Skillet & mixing bowl

Serves: Variable—2-3 eggs per person

Estimated preparation time: 10-15 minutes

INGREDIENTS	BASIC STEPS
3 eggs salt and pepper	1. Break 3 eggs into a bowl. Salt and pepper to taste. Mix well with a fork. Set aside.
1 teaspoon onion 1 teaspoon green pepper	2. Finely chop 1 teaspoon onion and 1 teaspoon green pepper.
1 tablespoon butter or margarine	3. Heat 1 tablespoon of butter or margarine in a skillet using medium-hot heat. Saute onions and peppers approximately 2-3 minutes.
3 tablespoons cottage cheese	4. Add another tablespoon of butter or margarine and blend in 3 tablespoons cottage cheese. When creamy, pour eggs into skillet.
	5. Scramble mixture until desired consistency is reached.
	6. Serve immediatey.

Notes:

Kitchen Tips
Virtually everyone will occasionally find himself wondering how to fish bits of egg shell out of a bowl of freshly cracked eggs. While most people try to grasp the piece between their thumb and forefinger it is much easier to scoop it up with a larger piece of shell.

Eggs Benedict

Difficulty rating: MODERATELY EASY

Serves: 4

Equipment needed: Blender & 2 skillets

Estimated preparation time: 20-25 minutes

INGREDIENTS

1 cup hollandaise sauce

2 tablespoons butter or margarine
4 slices Canadian bacon or ham

2 English muffins

4 eggs

paprika

BASIC STEPS

1. Open a jar of hollandaise sauce or prepare your own according to directions on page 198.

2. Heat 2 tablespoons butter or margarine and saute 4 slices Canadian bacon or ham for 4-5 minutes. Drain and keep warm in oven.

3. Split 2 English muffins and toast. Keep warm in oven.

4. Heat 1½ to 2 inches of water in a saucepan to boiling and then lower heat to simmer. Break 4 eggs, one at a time, into a saucer and then slip gently into the water. Cook 3-5 minutes and remove with a slotted spatula.

5. Cover each muffin half with a slice of Canadian bacon and top with a poached egg.

6. Spoon hollandaise sauce over eggs, sprinkle with paprika and serve.

Notes:

Onion and Pepper Frittata

Difficulty rating: MODERATELY
EASY

Equipment needed: Large skillet

Serves: 4-6

Estimated preparation time:
30 minutes

INGREDIENTS	BASIC STEPS
1 onion 1 green pepper ½ cup fresh chopped parsely small jar pimiento peppers	1. Chop 1 onion and 1 green pepper. Also, chop ½ cup fresh parsely and 1 small jar pimiento peppers.
2 tablespoons butter or margarine	2. Heat 2 tablespoons butter or margarine in a large skillet and saute onions and peppers 5-6 minutes.
¼ teaspoon thyme ¼ teaspoon basil	3. Add in the parsely and the pimientos together with ¼ teaspoon thyme and ¼ teaspoon basil.
6 eggs salt and pepper	4. In a bowl, beat 6 eggs and pour over the evenly distributed ingredients in the skillet. Salt and pepper to taste. Cover and turn heat to lowest setting. Cook for 12-15 minutes until the top surface of the frittata begins to firm up.
	5. Remove from heat and cover the top of the skillet with the eating surface of a large dinner plate. Invert skillet so frittata drops on the plate. Slide the frittata back into the skillet and cook other side 4-5 minutes.
	6. Transfer the frittata to a large dinner plate using the same procedure described in step 5.

French Toast

Difficulty rating: EASY

Equipment needed: Skillet or griddle & mixing bowl

Serves: 2-3

Estimated preparation time: 15-20 minutes

INGREDIENTS	BASIC STEPS
2 eggs ½ cup milk ⅛ teaspoon vanilla 1 teaspoon sugar	1. Break 2 eggs into a small mixing bowl. Add ½ cup milk, ⅛ teaspoon vanilla and 1 tablespoon sugar. Beat this mixture together.
1 tablespoon butter	2. Heat 1 tablespoon butter in a skillet or griddle using hot heat.
6-8 slices bread (whole wheat or white)	3. Soak each slice of bread on both sides and grill in the skillet or griddle until brown on both sides.
cinnamon powdered sugar	4. Remove to cutting board, cut each slice diagonally. Arrange on serving plate. Sprinkle with cinnamon or powdered sugar as desired.
syrup	5. Serve with choice of syrup.

Notes:

Kitchen Tips✓
Most everyone will drop an egg from time to time. Should this happen to you, simply cover the splotch with some salt, wait a few minutes, and sweep up the residue.

Pancakes

Difficulty rating: EASY

Equipment needed: Skillet or griddle & 2 mixing bowls

Serves: 2-3

Estimated preparation time: 20-30 minutes

INGREDIENTS

1¼ cups all-purpose flour
2 teaspoons baking powder
¼ teaspoon salt

1 egg
1 cup milk
1 tablespoon vegetable oil
1 tablespoon sugar

syrup, jelly or honey

BASIC STEPS

1. Combine in a bowl 1¼ cups flour, 2 teaspoons baking powder and ¼ teaspoon salt.

2. In a separate bowl, beat 1 egg well and add 1 cup milk, 1 tablespoon vegetable oil and 1 tablespoon sugar.

3. Blend the two mixtures together and let stand for 5-10 minutes.

4. Grease heated griddle. Test griddle by sprinkling a few drops of water on surface. If droplets "bounce" or "dance" the heat is just right. Pour batter onto griddle in uniform amounts (a ¼ cup measure is good) and cook until top surface is full of bubbles. Turn and brown other side.

5. Serve with favorite syrup, jelly or honey.

Notes:

Buckwheat Pancakes

Difficulty rating: EASY

Equipment needed: 2 mixing bowls & griddle or skillet

Serves: 3-4

Estimated preparation time: 20-30 minutes

INGREDIENTS

1   cup buckwheat flour
¼   cup whole wheat flour
¼   cup wheat germ
1   tablespoon baking powder

1½ cups milk
2   tablespoons vegetable oil
3   tablespoons sugar
2   lightly beaten eggs

syrup, jelly or honey

BASIC STEPS

1. Combine in a large mixing bowl, 1 cup buckwheat flour, ¼ cup whole wheat flour, ¼ cup wheat germ and 1 tablespoon baking powder.

2. In a separate bowl, blend together 1½ cups milk, 2 tablespoons vegetable oil, 3 tablespoons sugar and 2 lightly beaten eggs.

3. Blend the two mixtures together and let stand 5-10 minutes.

4. Grease heated griddle. Test griddle by sprinkling a few drops of water on surface. If droplets "bounce" or "dance" the heat is just right. Pour batter onto griddle in uniform amounts (a ¼ cup measure is good) and cook until top surface is full of bubbles. Turn and brown the other side.

5. Serve with favorite syrup, jelly or honey.

Notes:

Cornmeal Griddle Cakes

Difficulty rating: EASY

Equipment needed: Skillet or griddle & 2 mixing bowls

Serves: 2-3

Estimated preparation time: 20-30 minutes

INGREDIENTS	BASIC STEPS
½ cup cornmeal ½ cup all-purpose flour 1 teaspoon baking powder ½ teaspoon salt	1. Combine together in a bowl, ½ cup cornmeal, ½ cup all-purpose flour, 1 teaspoon baking powder and ½ teaspoon salt.
1 egg 1 cup buttermilk 1 tablespoon sugar	2. In a separate bowl, beat 1 egg and add to this 1 cup buttermilk and 1 tablespoon sugar.
	3. Blend the two mixtures together and let stand for 5-10 minutes.
	4. Grease heated griddle. Test griddle by sprinkling a few drops of water on surface. If droplets "bounce" or "dance" the heat is just right. Pour batter onto griddle in uniform amounts (a ¼ cup measure is good) and cook until top surface is full of bubbles. Turn and brown other side.
Syrup, jelly or honey	5. Serve with favorite syrup, jelly or honey.

Notes:

Blueberry Muffins

Difficulty rating: EASY

Serves: Yields 12 muffins

Equipment needed: Twelve-unit muffin pan & mixing bowl

Estimated preparation time: 30-40 minutes

INGREDIENTS

1 cup fresh blueberries

3 cups whole wheat flour
1 tablespoon baking powder
½ cup sugar
½ teaspoon salt

2 eggs
¼ cup vegetable oil
1 cup buttermilk

BASIC STEPS

1. Preheat oven to 400°.

2. Wash 1 cup fresh blueberries.

3. In a bowl, combine 3 cups whole wheat flour, 1 tablespoon baking powder, ½ cup sugar and ½ teaspoon salt.

4. In a separate bowl, beat 2 eggs and add in ¼ cup vegetable oil and 1 cup buttermilk. Pour this mixture into the bowl containing the dry ingredients. Stir well and mix in the fresh blueberries.

5. Spoon into a greased twelve-unit muffin pan, filling each cup about ⅔ full.

6. Bake for 20 minutes.

Notes:

Corn Muffins

Difficulty rating: EASY

Equipment needed: 2 mixing bowls & twelve-unit muffin pan

Serves: Yields 12 muffins

Estimated preparation time: 30-35 minutes

INGREDIENTS

1 cup cornmeal
1 cup whole wheat flour
2 teaspoons baking powder

1 cup milk
½ cup honey
¼ cup melted butter or margarine
1 lightly beaten egg

BASIC STEPS

1. Preheat oven to 400°

2. In a bowl, combine 1 cup corn meal, 1 cup whole wheat flour and 2 teaspoons baking powder.

3. Blend together in a bowl 1 cup milk, ½ cup honey, ¼ cup butter or margarine and 1 lightly beaten egg.

4. Combine the two mixtures and stir gently.

5. Oil a twelve-unit muffin pan and fill each cup ⅔ full. Place in oven and bake for 20 minutes.

Notes:

Quick Coffee Cake

Difficulty rating: EASY

Equipment needed: 1 9x9 inch baking pan & mixing bowls

Serves: 4-5

Estimated preparation time: 50-60 minutes

INGREDIENTS

½ cup chopped walnuts or pecans
1 teaspoon cinnamon
½ teaspoon nutmeg
¼ cup brown sugar

1½ cups all-purpose flour
1 cup sugar
2 teaspoons baking powder
½ teaspoon baking soda

1 cup sour cream
2 eggs

BASIC STEPS

1. Preheat oven to 350º.

2. Chop ½ cup walnuts or pecans. Place in a small bowl and add in 1 teaspoon cinnamon, ½ teaspoon nutmeg and ¼ cup brown sugar. Mix well.

3. In a bowl, combine 1½ cups all-purpose flour, 1 cup sugar, 2 teaspoons baking powder and ½ teaspoon baking soda.

4. Mix together in a separate bowl 1 cup sour cream and 2 well beaten eggs.

5. Blend the flour and sour cream mixtures together and pour into a 9"x 9" greased pan. Sprinkle the nutmeg and brown sugar mix over the top and bake for 35-40 minutes.

Notes:

Apple Coffee Cake

Difficulty rating: EASY

Equipment needed: twelve-cup tube pan & 2 mixing bowls

Serves: 10-12

Estimated preparation time: 60-75 minutes

INGREDIENTS

2 cups apples
1 cup English walnuts

3 eggs
1 cup vegetable oil
1½ cups honey

2 cups all-purpose flour
1 teaspoon salt
1 teaspoon baking soda
1 teaspoon baking powder
1 teaspoon cinnamon

powdered sugar

BASIC STEPS

1. Preheat oven at 350º.

2. Slice 2 cups of apples into small pieces and chop 1 cup English walnuts.

3. In a bowl, beat 3 eggs and combine with 1 cup vegetable oil and 1½ cups honey.

4. In a separate bowl, mix together 2 cups all-purpose flour, 1 teaspoon salt, 1 teaspoon baking soda, 1 teaspoon baking powder and 1 teaspoon cinnamon.

5. Blend the two mixtures together and fold in the apples and walnuts.

6. Transfer to greased tube pan and bake for 45-50 minutes.

7. Cool, remove from pan, and sprinkle with powdered sugar.

Notes:

Sour Cream Coffee Cake

Difficulty rating: EASY

Equipment needed: 2 mixing bowls & twelve-cup tube pan

Serves: 6-8

Estimated preparation time: 75-80 minutes

INGREDIENTS

1 cup English walnuts
½ cup sugar
2 teaspoons cinnamon

2¼ cups all-purpose flour
1 teaspoon baking powder
½ teaspoon baking soda

2 eggs
1 cup butter or margarine
1 cup honey
1 cup sour cream
1 teaspoon vanilla

powdered sugar

BASIC STEPS

1. Preheat oven at 350°.

2. Chop 1 cup English walnuts and mix together with ½ cup sugar and 2 teaspoons cinnamon.

3. In a large mixing bowl, combine 2¼ cups all-purpose flour, 1 teaspoon baking powder and ½ teaspoon baking soda.

4. In a separate bowl, beat 2 eggs and add in 1 cup softened butter or margarine, 1 cup honey, 1 cup sour cream and 1 teaspoon vanilla.

5. Add the liquid mixture to the dry ingredients and mix thoroughly.

6. Pour one-half of the batter into a lightly greased tube pan. Sprinkle walnut mixture on the batter and fill in the remaining batter.

7. Bake for 1 hour. Sprinkle with powdered sugar when cooled.

Notes:

Using Garnishes

Garnishes add a nice touch to a meal so why not put your creative talents to work with some of the ones listed below.

Parsley sprigs
Lettuce leaves
Spinach leaves
Watercress
Scallions
Cucumber slices
Paprika
Maraschino cherries
Lemon wedges
Onion rings

Olives
Nuts
Pimentos
Celery sticks
Green pepper rings
Carrot curls
Cherry tomatoes
Orange wedges
Spiced apple rings

Soups, Salads
and
Sandwiches

French Onion Soup

Difficulty rating: EASY

Equipment needed: Large kettle

Serves: 4

Estimated preparation time: 25-30 minutes

INGREDIENTS

4 onions

2-3 tablespoons butter or margarine

3 cans (10½ ounces) condensed beef broth
1 teaspoon Worcestershire sauce
salt and pepper

1 loaf French bread
½ cup grated Parmesan cheese

grated Parmesan cheese

BASIC STEPS

1. Slice 4 onions.

2. Heat 2-3 tablespoons butter or margarine in a large kettle and saute onions for 10-15 minutes until lightly browned.

3. Add in 3 cans (10½ ounces) condensed beef broth and 1 teaspoon Worcestershire sauce. Bring to a boil and then reduce heat and let simmer. Salt and pepper to taste.

4. Slice 4 pieces of French bread, butter and sprinkle with Parmesan cheese. Place the bread under a broiler until cheese has browned slightly.

5. Ladle soup into bowls and float a piece of the bread on the soup.

6. Garnish with a sprinkling of Parmesan cheese and serve.

Notes:

Vegetable Soup

Difficulty rating: EASY

Equipment needed: Large kettle

Serves: 10-12

Estimated preparation time:
2½ to 3 hours, approximately 2 hours of which is cooking time.

INGREDIENTS

½ head cabbage
3 potatoes
2 ribs celery
2 carrots

1½ quarts water
4 beef bouillon cubes

1 package (10 ounces) frozen whole kernel corn
1 can (28 ounces) whole tomatoes
½ cup barley
½ cup red wine
1 bay leaf

1 teaspoon tarragon
½ teaspoon thyme
½ teaspoon marjoram
salt and pepper

BASIC STEPS

1. Shred ½ head cabbage and cut 3 potatoes, 2 ribs celery, and 2 carrots into bite size pieces.

2. In a large kettle, mix together 1½ quarts water and 4 beef bouillon cubes.

3. Place the vegetables into the water and add in 1 package (10 ounces)frozen whole kernel corn, 1 can (28 ounces) whole tomatoes, ½ cup barley, ½ cup red wine and 1 bay leaf.

4. Flavor with 1 teaspoon tarragon, ½ teaspoon thyme and ½ teaspoon marjoram. Salt and pepper to taste.

5. Bring soup to boil and then simmer until vegetables are barely done (about 1½ to 2 hours). Add more water if needed.

6. Serve with warm homemade bread.

Notes:

Vegetable-Beef Soup

Difficulty rating: EASY

Equipment needed: Large kettle & skillet

Serves: 12-14

Estimated preparation time:
2½ to 3 hours, approximately 2 hours of which is cooking time.

INGREDIENTS	BASIC STEPS
3-4 pounds beef shank	1. Heat 2 tablespoons vegetable oil in a skillet and brown 3-4 pounds of beef shank.
½ head cabbage 3 potatoes 2 ribs celery 2 carrots	2. Shred ½ head cabbage and cut 3 potatoes, 2 ribs celery and 2 carrots into bite size pieces.
1½ quarts water	3. Pour 1½ quarts of water into a large kettle and add in the beef shank and vegetables.
1 package (10 ounces) frozen whole kernel corn 1 can (28 ounces) whole tomatoes ½ cup barley ½ cup red wine 1 bay leaf	4. Mix in 1 package (10 ounces) frozen whole kernel corn, 1 can (28 ounces) whole tomatoes, ½ cup barley, ½ cup red wine and 1 bay leaf.
1 teaspoon tarragon ½ teaspoon thyme ½ teaspoon marjoram salt and pepper	5. Flavor with 1 teaspoon tarragon, ½ teaspoon thyme and 1 teaspoon marjoram. Salt and pepper to taste.
	6. Bring soup to a boil and then simmer until vegetables are barely done (about 1½ to 2 hours). Add more water if needed.
	7. Serve with warm homemade bread.

Notes:

Crab Bisque

Difficulty rating: VERY EASY

Equipment needed: Three-quart saucepan

Serves: 4

Estimated preparation time: 20-30 minutes

INGREDIENTS

- 1 can (10¾ ounces) tomato soup
- 1 can (10¾ ounces) cream of mushroom soup
- 1½ cups half & half cream
- 1 cup picked crab meat

- 1 tablespoon parsely
- ½ teaspoon paprika
- 2 teaspoons dry sherry
  salt and pepper

BASIC STEPS

1. In a saucepan, combine 1 can (10¾ ounces) tomato soup, 1 can (10¾ ounces) cream of mushroom soup, 1½ cups half & half cream and 1 cup picked crab meat.

2. Flavor with 1 tablespoon parsely, ½ teaspoon paprika and 2 teaspoons dry sherry. Salt and pepper to taste and let simmer for 25-20 minutes.

3. Serve hot.

Notes:

Clam Chowder
(New England Style)

Difficulty rating: EASY

Serves: 4-6

Equipment needed: Large saucepan & skillet

Estimated preparation time: 45-60 minutes

INGREDIENTS

1 onion
2 cups potatoes

⅓ cup salt pork

2 cans (7½ ounces each) minced clams
1 cup milk
⅔ cup light cream
salt and pepper

BASIC STEPS

1. Chop 1 onion and cut 2 cups potatoes into bite size pieces.

2. Cut into small pieces ⅓ cup salt pork.

3. In a skillet, fry the salt pork until crisp and add in the onions and saute for 5 minutes.

4. Add the potatoes and just enough water to cover ingredients. Cover and let cook for 15-20 minutes until potatoes are tender.

5. Transfer ingredients to a large saucepan and add 2 cans (7½ ounces each) minced clams, 1 cup milk and ⅔ cup light cream. Salt and pepper to taste and let simmer for 10 minutes.

Notes:

Fish Chowder

Difficulty rating: EASY

Equipment needed: Large kettle

Serves: 5-7

Estimated preparation time: 40-45 minutes

INGREDIENTS

2 onions
5 potatoes

2 tablespoons butter or margarine
2½ cups water
¼ teaspoon Tabasco sauce

1½ pounds fish fillets (fresh or frozen)

2 cups milk
1 cup evaporated milk
1 can (16 ounces) whole kernel corn
salt and pepper

paprika

BASIC STEPS

1. Slice 2 onions and peel and cut 5 potatoes into bite size pieces.

2. Melt 2 tablespoons butter or margarine in a large soup kettle over medium heat and saute onions approximately 5 minutes. Add 2½ cups water, ¼ teaspoon Tabasco sauce and the potaotes.

3. Thaw and slice fish fillets into 2-3 inch pieces and add to kettle. Cover and let simmer for 25 minutes.

4. Add 2 cups milk, 1 cup evaporated milk, and 1 can (16 ounces) corn. Salt and pepper to taste. Continue to heat to eating temperature.

5. Scoop into serving bowls, sprinkle with paprika and serve.

Notes:

Cheddar Cheese Soup

Difficulty rating: EASY

Equipment needed: Large saucepan & grater

Serves: 4

Estimated preparation time: 15-20 minutes

INGREDIENTS

3 tablespoons butter or margarine
⅓ cup all-purpose flour

2 cups milk
1½ cups grated cheddar cheese
1 chicken bouillon cube and 1 cup water
   salt and pepper

   croutons

BASIC STEPS

1. Melt 3 tablespoons butter or margarine in a saucepan and stir in ⅓ cup all-purpose flour.

2. Blend in 2 cups milk, 1½ cups grated cheddar cheese and 1 cup chicken bouillon. Simmer until cheese has melted. Salt and pepper to taste.

3. Serve hot with a sprinkling of croutons.

Notes:

Kitchen Tips ✓
In reheating soup, separate out only the amount that is needed for the immediate meal. Reheating the total volume several times will result in overcooking.

Celery-Cheese Soup

Difficulty rating: EASY

Serves: 4

Equipment needed: Three-quart saucepan, skillet & grater

Estimated preparation time: 30-40 minutes

INGREDIENTS	BASIC STEPS
1 onion 3 ribs celery	1. Chop 1 onion and 3 ribs celery.
2 tablespoons butter or margarine 1 cup water 3 cups milk	2. Heat 2 tablespoons butter or margarine in a skillet and saute onions and celery for 5 minutes. Add 1 cup water and 3 cups milk. Let simmer for 20 minutes.
1 tablespoon cornstarch 2 tablespoons Worcestershire sauce 2 cups grated cheddar cheese salt and pepper	3. Blend in 1 tablespoon cornstarch, 2 tablespoons Worcestershire sauce and 2 cups grated cheddar cheese. Heat through and salt and pepper to taste.
paprika	4. Garnish with sprinkling of paprika and serve.

Notes:

Kitchen Tips 🗸
Before refrigerating cheese, wrap it in a cloth soaked in vinegar and seal in plastic wrap. This will keep it from becoming dry and hard.

Creamed Tomato-Celery Soup

Difficulty rating: MODERATELY EASY

Equipment needed: Blender, saucepan & skillet

Serves: 4-6

Estimated preparation time:
75-85 minutes, approximately 65 minutes of which is cooking time.

INGREDIENTS

1 onion
6 ribs celery
3 cups tomatoes

2 tablespoons vegetable oil

5 chicken bouillon cubes & five cups water
1 teaspoon tarragon

1 tablespoon butter
½ cup all-purpose flour
1⅓ cups milk

salt and pepper

1 cup half & half cream

BASIC STEPS

1. Chop 1 onion and 6 ribs of celery. Also, peel and chop 3 cups tomatoes.

2. Heat 2 tablespoons vegetable oil in a skillet and saute onions and celery for 5 minutes.

3. Add in the tomatoes, 5 cups of chicken bouillon and 1 teaspoon tarragon. Cover and let simmer for 45-50 minutes.

4. Remove from heat and let cool. Transfer contents to a blender and puree until smooth.

5. In a saucepan, melt 1 tablespoon butter and gradually stir in ½ cup all-purpose flour and 1⅓ cups milk. Simmer and stir until thick.

6. Mix in the pureed vegetables and let simmer for 12-15 minutes. Salt and pepper to taste.

7. Blend in 1 cup half & half cream, heat through and serve.

Notes:

Quick Vichyssoise

Difficulty rating: VERY EASY

Equipment needed: Blender & grater

Serves: 4

Estimated preparation time: 10-15 minutes

INGREDIENTS

¼ teaspoon grated onion

1 can (20 ounces) vichyssoise
1 cup sour cream
   salt and pepper

2 tablespoons chopped chives

BASIC STEPS

1. Grate ¼ teaspoon onion.

2. Combine the onion, 1 can (20 ounces) vichyssoise, and 1 cup sour cream in a blender and puree. Salt and pepper to taste.

3. Serve chilled with a sprinkling of chopped chives.

Notes:

Gazpacho

Difficulty rating: VERY EASY

Equipment needed: Blender

Serves: 3-4

Estimated preparation time:
10-15 minutes

INGREDIENTS

2 cups tomatoes
½ cup onion
½ cup green pepper

¼ cup red wine
¼ teaspoon garlic salt
1 tablespoon olive oil
2 tablespoons lemon juice
½ teaspoon paprika
 salt and pepper

 croutons

BASIC STEPS

1. Peel and chop two cups tomatoes, ½ cup onions and ½ cup green pepper.

2. In a blender, combine the chopped vegetables with ¼ cup red wine, ¼ teaspoon garlic salt, 1 tablespoon olive oil, 2 tablespoons lemon juice and ½ teaspoon paprika. Blend until smooth. Salt and pepper to taste.

3. Chill at least 1 hour and serve with croutons.

Notes:

Kitchen Tips
Here are two tips for peeling tomatoes:
(1) Run a fork through the stem end and hold the tomato over a flame. This will split the skin and make it easier to peel.
(2) Place the tomato in boiling water for 45-60 seconds and then transfer to a bowl of ice water. This will loosen the skin and make removing it a cinch.

Cold Avocado Soup

Difficulty rating: VERY EASY

Equipment needed: Blender

Serves: 4-6

Estimated preparation time:
10-15 minutes

INGREDIENTS

1 avocado

3 cups milk
1 cup sour cream
½ teaspoon tarragon
¼ teaspoon basil
¼ teaspoon oregano
salt and pepper

4-6 breadsticks

BASIC STEPS

1. Peel and cut into small pieces 1 avocado

2. In a blender, combine the avocado with 3 cups milk, 1 cup sour cream, ½ teaspoon tarragon, ¼ teaspoon basil and ¼ teaspoon oregano. Puree until smooth. Salt and pepper to taste.

3. Serve chilled with breadsticks.

Notes:

Antipasto

Difficulty rating: VERY EASY

Equipment needed: Large serving platter

Serves: 6-8

Estimated preparation time: 30-40 minutes

INGREDIENTS	BASIC STEPS
1 head lettuce 2 tomatoes 2 green peppers	1. Wash and tear the leaves from 1 head of lettuce, quarter 2 tomatoes and slice 2 green peppers.
6 slices boiled ham 1 jar pimiento peppers 6-8 slices salami 6 slices prosciutto 6-8 slices Mozzarella cheese ½ pound Italian Fontina cheese 2 jars artichoke hearts 1 can anchovies black and green olives	2. Arrange the lettuce leaves on a large platter and cover decoratively with the following: 6 slices boiled ham, 1 jar pimiento peppers, 6-8 slices salami, 6 slices prosciutto, 6-8 slices Mozzarella cheese, ½ pound Italian Fontina cheese cut into smaller squares, 2 jars artichoke hearts, 1 can anchovies, assorted black and green olives and the tomatoes and peppers prepared in step 1.
Italian salad dressing oil and vinegar	3. Serve with Italian salad dressing and/or oil and vinegar.

Notes:

Kitchen Tips
Cheese can be cut much more easily with a warm knife.

Greek Salad

Difficulty rating: EASY

Equipment needed: Large mixing bowl

Serves: 4-5

Estimated preparation time: 20-30 minutes

INGREDIENTS

⅓ cup olive oil
1½ tablespoons white vinegar
1 teaspoon thyme
1 teaspoon marjoram
1 teaspoon tarragon
1 teaspoon sugar
   salt and pepper

4 scallions

1 head romaine lettuce
6-8 radishes
4 tomatoes
6-8 black olives
½ pound feta cheese
1 can anchovies

   chopped parsley
   pepper

BASIC STEPS

1. In a small mixing bowl, blend together ⅓ cup olive oil, 1½ tablespoons white vinegar, 1 teaspoon thyme, 1 teaspoon marjoram and 1 teaspoon tarragon. Also, add in 1 teaspoon sugar. Salt and pepper to taste.

2. Chop 4 scallions and add to dressing mixture. Mix thoroughly.

3. Wash and tear the leaves from 1 head romaine lettuce. Slice 6-8 radishes, peel and quarter 4 tomatoes, cut 6-8 black olives in half and cut ½ pound feta cheese into 1 inch cubes. Also, open a can of anchovies.

4. Tear the lettuce leaves into smaller pieces and line the bottom of a large plate. Arrange the radishes, tomatoes, black olives, feta cheese and anchovies decoratively over the lettuce. Sprinkle with chopped parsley and pepper.

5. Distribute the dressing evenly over the ingredients on the plate and serve.

Notes:

Waldorf Salad

Difficulty rating: VERY EASY

Equipment needed: Mixing bowl

Serves: 4

Estimated preparation time:
10-15 minutes

INGREDIENTS

2 apples
1 cup celery
½ cup English walnuts

⅓-½ cup mayonnaise

lettuce
paprika

BASIC STEPS

1. Cut 2 apples into bite size pieces and chop 1 cup celery and ½ cup English walnuts.

2. Combine these ingredients in a bowl and mix thoroughly with ⅓ to ½ cup mayonnaise.

3. Serve on a plate over a leaf of lettuce and sprinkle with paprika.

Notes:

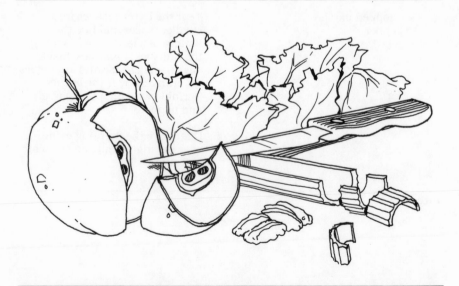

Tossed Salad

Difficulty rating: VERY EASY

Equipment needed: Large bowl & grater

Serves: 4

Estimated preparation time: 20 minutes

INGREDIENTS

1 head of lettuce

½ cucumber
2 ribs celery
4-6 scallions
½ green pepper
4 tomatoes
1 carrot

assorted salad dressings

BASIC STEPS

1. Wash 1 head of lettuce and tear into small pieces.

2. Chop ½ cucumber, 2 ribs celery, 4-6 scallions and ½ green pepper. Also, quarter 4 tomatoes and peel and grate 1 carrot.

3. Mix all ingredients together in a large bowl. Toss well.

4. Serve with a selection of salad dressings.

Notes:

Kitchen Tips ✓
Vegetables and fruits will stay fresher longer if you cover the bottom of the vegetable compartment in your refrigerator with paper towels.

Wilted Lettuce

Difficulty rating: EASY

Equipment needed: Skillet & bowl

Serves: 4

Estimated preparation time: 10-15 minutes

INGREDIENTS

1 head lettuce

4 slices bacon

¼ cup water
½ cup vinegar
2 tablespoons brown sugar
1 teaspoon lemon juice
½ teaspoon salt
⅛ teaspoon pepper

BASIC STEPS

1. Wash and break into smaller pieces 1 head of lettuce. Drain and transfer to a serving bowl.

2. Cut 4 slices of bacon into small bits.

3. In a skillet, fry bacon bits until nicely brown.

4. To the bacon add ¼ cup water, ½ cup vinegar, 2 tablespoons brown sugar, 1 teaspoon lemon juice, ½ teaspoon salt and ⅛ teaspoon pepper.

5. Bring to boil, pour over the lettuce and serve immediately.

Notes:

Three Bean Salad

Difficulty rating: VERY EASY

Equipment needed: 2 mixing bowls & three-quart saucepan

Serves: 6

Estimated preparation time: 20-30 minutes

INGREDIENTS

1½ cups vinegar
1½ cups sugar
⅓ cup water
1 teaspoon salt

6-8 scallions
1 jar pimiento peppers
1 can (16 ounces) green string beans
1 can (16 ounces) yellow wax beans
1 can (16 ounces) kidney beans

BASIC STEPS

1. In a 3-quart saucepan, combine 1½ cups vinegar, 1½ cups sugar, ⅓ cup water and 1 teaspoon salt. Bring to a boil and cook for 5 minutes. Let cool.

2. Finely chop 6-8 scallions and 1 jar pimiento peppers. Open 1 can (16 ounces) of green string beans, 1 can (16 ounces) yellow wax beans and 1 can (16 ounces) kidney beans.

3. Combine the beans, scallions, and piminentos and cover with the syrup.

4. Chill and serve.

Notes:

Lima Bean and Bacon Salad

Difficulty rating: EASY

Equipment needed: Skillet, one-quart saucepan & 2 mixing bowls

Serves: 4

Estimated preparation time: 20-30 minutes

INGREDIENTS

2 packages (10 ounces) frozen baby lima beans

6 slices bacon

1 clove of garlic

¼ cup olive oil
2 tablespoons lemon juice
pepper

2 tablespoons chopped parsley

BASIC STEPS

1. Cook 2 packages (10 ounces each) frozen baby lima beans. Drain and let cool.

2. Fry 6 slices bacon until crisp. Drain on a paper towel.

3. Slice a garlic clove in half and rub the inside of a salad bowl with the cut side of the clove. Discard the garlic.

4. Combine in a separate bowl, ¼ cup olive oil and 2 tablespoons lemon juice. Mix thoroughly and add pepper according to taste.

5. Crumple the bacon and mix with the baby limas in the bowl rubbed with garlic. Pour the olive oil and lemon dressing on the bean mixture and toss until everything is evenly coated.

6. Chill and serve with a sprinkling of chopped parsley.

Notes:

Kitchen Tips✓
A 16 ounce can of vegetables yields approximately the same amount as a 10 ounce frozen package of the same vegetable.

Cauliflower and Sardine Salad

Difficulty rating: EASY

Serves: 4

Equipment needed: Three-quart saucepan, mixing bowl & grater

Estimated preparation time: 20-30 minutes

INGREDIENTS

2 packages (10 ounces each) frozen cauliflower

15 black olives
½ cup onions

2 tablespoons capers
1 can sardines

French or Italian dressing

BASIC STEPS

1. Cook 2 packages (10 ounces each) frozen cauliflower. Drain and let cool.

2. Slice 15 black olives and grate ½ cup onions.

3. When cauliflower has cooled, break into florets.

4. In a mixing bowl, combine the cauliflower florets, black olives, grated onions, 2 tablespoons capers and 1 can sardines.

5. Chill and serve with French or Italian dressing.

Notes:

Crunchy Coleslaw Salad

Difficulty rating: EASY

Equipment needed: Grater & mixing bowl

Serves: 4

Estimated preparation time: 15-20 minutes

INGREDIENTS

½ head of cabbage
1 tablespoon onion
⅓ cup English walnuts

½ cup whipping cream
¼ cup sour cream
2 teaspoons French-style mustard
2 tablespoons lemon juice
1 teaspoon sugar
salt and pepper

BASIC STEPS

1. Shred ½ head of cabbage and finely chop 1 tablespoon onion and ⅓ cup English walnuts. Mix thoroughly in a bowl.

2. In a separate bowl, blend together ½ cup whipping cream, ¼ cup sour cream, 2 teaspoons French-style mustard, 2 tablespoons lemon juice and 1 teaspoon sugar. Salt and pepper to taste.

3. Pour the dressing over the shredded cabbage mixture and toss until everything is evenly coated.

4. Chill before serving.

Notes:

Lima Bean Salad

Difficulty rating: VERY EASY

Serves: 4

Equipment needed: Mixing bowl, colander & saucepan

Estimated preparation time: 20-25 minutes

INGREDIENTS	BASIC STEPS
1 package (10 ounces) frozen lima beans	1. Cook 1 package (10 ounces) frozen lima beans. Drain in a colander and set aside until cooled to room temperature.
1 onion ½ cup mushrooms	2. Slice 1 onion and ½ cup mushrooms.
¼ cup salad oil 2 tablespoons vinegar	3. Mix together in a jar, ¼ cup salad oil and 2 tablespoons vinegar.
salt and pepper	4. Combine the lima beans, onions and mushrooms and toss well with the oil and vinegar mixture. Salt and pepper to taste.
	5. Serve as a side dish.

Notes:

Fruit Salad

Difficulty rating: VERY EASY

Serves: 4

Equipment needed: Saucepan & large mixing bowl

Estimated preparation time: 20-30 minutes

INGREDIENTS	BASIC STEPS
1¼ cups water ½ cup sugar	1. In a saucepan, mix together over low heat 1¼ cups water and ½ cup sugar. Bring to a boil and cook for 4-5 minutes.
1 tablespoon lemon juice 2 tablespoons Grand Marnier or Cointreau liqueur	2. Let cool and add 1 tablespoon lemon juice and 2 tablespoons Grand Marnier or Cointreau liqueur.
2 bananas 2 apples 1 pear 1 peach 1 orange ½ melon ½ cup grapes	3. In the meantime slice 2 bananas, 2 apples, 1 pear and 1 peach. Also, section 1 orange, cut the fruit from ½ of a melon into bite size pieces and measure out ½ cup of grapes.
	4. Put all the fruit in a large bowl and cover with the syrup.
4 maraschino cherries	5. Let marinate for 2 hours and serve in bowls garnished with a maraschino cherry if you like.

Notes:

Kitchen Tips
A good way to keep freshly cut apples and bananas from discoloring is to lightly sprinkle them with lemon juice.

Peach-Cottage Cheese Salad

Difficulty rating: VERY EASY

Equipment needed: Mixing bowl

Serves: 2

Estimated preparation time:
5-10 minutes

INGREDIENTS	BASIC STEPS
2 cups cottage cheese ¼ cup mayonnaise	1. Blend together in a bowl, 2 cups cottage cheese and ¼ cup mayonnaise.
1 head of lettuce	2. Line the edge of 2 salad plates with lettuce.
peach slices (fresh or canned)	3. Place ½ of the cottage cheese mixture in the center of each plate and top with peach slices (fresh or canned).
nutmeg walnut halves (optional)	4. Sprinkle lightly with nutmeg and garnish with walnut halves if you like.

Notes:

Melon-Avocado Salad

Difficulty rating: VERY EASY

Equipment needed: 2 mixing bowls & melon scoop

Serves: 4

Estimated preparation time: 15-20 minutes

INGREDIENTS

2 avocados

½ honeydew melon

½ cup olive oil
2 tablespoons lemon juice
½ teaspoon salt
¼ teaspoon pepper
¼ teaspoon tarragon

lettuce leaves

BASIC STEPS

1. Cut 2 avocados in half and remove pits. Using a melon scoop, dig out the flesh in the form of little balls and place in a mixing bowl.

2. Following this same procedure, scoop out ½ honeydew melon. Mix the melon and avocado balls together.

3. In a separate bowl, combine ½ cup olive oil, 2 tablespoons lemon juice, ½ teaspoon salt, ¼ teaspoon pepper and ¼ teaspoon tarragon. Mix well.

4. Pour the liquid mixture over the avocado and melon balls and toss until well coated.

5. Serve chilled on lettuce leaves.

Notes:

Melon Salad

Difficulty rating: VERY EASY

Serves: 3-4

Equipment needed: Large bowl &
2 small bowls

Estimated preparation time:
25-30 minutes

INGREDIENTS

½ cup walnuts
¼ cup raisins

¼ cup French salad dressing
½ teaspoon French-style
mustard
2 tablespoons whipping cream
2 tablespoons finely chopped
parsely

½ honeydew melon or cantelope

1 container (16 ounces) cottage
cheese
1 head lettuce

BASIC STEPS

1. Chop ½ cup walnuts and mix
together in a bowl with ¼ cup
raisins.

2. Blend together in a bowl, ¼ cup
French salad dressing, ½
teaspoon French-style mustard,
2 tablespoons whipping cream
and 2 tablespoons finely chopped
parsely.

3. Cut into bite size pieces ½ of a
honeydew melon or cantelope.

4. Combine the walnut-raisin mix,
the dressing and the melon
pieces. Mix well and let stand for
20-30 minutes.

5. Serve on a bed of lettuce with a
scoop of cottage cheese.

Notes:

Hamburgers

Difficulty rating: VERY EASY

Equipment needed: Skillet & bowl

Serves: 4

Estimated preparation time: 10-15 minutes

INGREDIENTS

1 pound ground beef
1 tablespoon dried onion flakes
1 tablespoon catsup

2 tablespoons butter or margarine

4 hamburger rolls

BASIC STEPS

1. In a bowl, mix together 1 pound ground beef, 1 tablespoon dried onion flakes and 1 tablespoon catsup.

2. Divide hamburger mixture into four equal parts and shape into patties.

3. Heat 2 tablespoons butter or margarine in a skillet and fry burgers over high heat for 2 minutes on each side. Reduce heat and cook for another 3-5 minutes on each side.

4. Serve on hamburger rolls, toasted or plain, with your favorite topping.

Notes:

Kitchen Tips ✓
For juicier hamburgers, cook both sides before salting

Reuben Sandwiches

Difficulty rating: EASY

Equipment needed: Skillet

Serves: 2

Estimated preparation time:
15-20 minutes

INGREDIENTS

2 slices dark rye bread
1 tablespoon butter

2 slices Swiss cheese
2 tablespoons sauerkraut
4 slices corned beef or pastrami

2 tablespoons Thousand Island
  dressing

2 slices dark rye bread
1 tablespoon butter

dill pickles

BASIC STEPS

1. Butter 2 slices of dark rye bread.

2. Place 1 slice of Swiss cheese, 1
   tablespoon sauerkraut and 2
   slices of corned beef or pastrami
   on each slice of bread.

3. Top the sandwich ingredients
   with 1 tablespoon of Thousand
   Island dressing.

4. Complete the sandwich with
   another slice of dark rye bread
   and butter the outside of both
   sandwiches.

5. Grill the sandwiches on both
   sides in a skillet until the cheese
   melts.

6. Serve with dill pickles.

Notes:

Cold Sandwich Platter

Difficulty rating: VERY EASY

Equipment needed: Large serving platter

Serves: 6-8

Estimated preparation time: 25-30 minutes

INGREDIENTS

2 tomatoes
1 cucumber
1 onion
½ cup black olives
1 head lettuce
6-8 scallions

1 pound Swiss cheese
½ pound salami
1 pound roast beef
1 can sardines

assorted breads

butter
pickles
horseradish
mustard
mayonnaise

BASIC STEPS

1. Slice 2 tomatoes, 1 cucumber, 1 onion and ½ cup black olives. Also, clean 1 head of lettuce and 6-8 scallions.

2. Cover a large serving platter with lettuce leaves and arrange the vegetables on the lettuce together with 1 pound sliced Swiss cheese, ½ pound sliced salami, 1 pound sliced roast beef and 1 can sardines.

3. On a separate plate arrange 4 slices rye, 4 slices whole wheat and 6 slices white bread. Or, if you prefer, use assorted rolls.

4. Serve with butter, pickles, horseradish, mustard and mayonnaise. Let everyone make his or her own sandwich.

Notes:

Broiled Open-Faced Tuna Sandwich

Difficulty rating: EASY

Equipment needed: Small mixing bowl

Serves: 3-5

Estimated preparation time: 15-20 minutes

INGREDIENTS

1 can (6½ or 7 ounces) tuna
2 tablespoons finely chopped onion
2 tablespoons chopped sweet pickle
¼ cup mayonnaise

3 English muffins

6 slices cheese

BASIC STEPS

1. In a bowl, mix together 1 can (6½ or 7 ounces) tuna, 2 tablespoons finely chopped onions, 2 tablespoons chopped sweet pickles and ¼ cup mayonnaise.

2. Cut 3 English muffins in half and toast.

3. Spread the tuna mixture over the 6 English muffin halves and top with slices of cheese.

4. Place the muffins under a broiler about 4-5 inches from heat source and cook until cheese melts (approximately 4-5 minutes).

5. Serve hot.

Notes:

Broiled Open-Faced
Cheese and Olive Sandwich

Difficulty rating: EASY

Equipment needed: Small mixing bowl & grater

Serves: 3-5

Estimated preparation time: 12-15 minutes

INGREDIENTS

½ cup green or black olives
¾ cup grated cheddar cheese
¼ cup mayonnaise
¼ teaspoon salt
¼ teaspoon curry powder

3 English muffins

BASIC STEPS

1. In a bowl, mix together ½ cup chopped green or black olives, ¾ cup grated cheddar cheese, ¼ cup mayonnaise, ¼ teaspoon salt and ¼ teaspoon curry powder.

2. Cut 3 English muffins in half and toast.

3. Spread the cheese and olive mixture over the 6 English muffin halves.

4. Place the muffins under a broiler about 4-5 inches from the heat source and cook until cheese melts (approximately 4-5 minutes).

5. Serve hot.

Notes:

Grilled Ham and Cheese Sandwich

Difficulty rating: EASY

Equipment needed: Skillet & grater

Serves: 2

Estimated preparation time: 15-20 minutes

INGREDIENTS

2 slices bread

½ pound grated Swiss or American cheese
2 slices ham
2 teaspoons French-style mustard or mayonnaise

2 slices bread

sweet pickles

BASIC STEPS

1. Butter 2 slices bread.

2. Cover each slice with a layer of grated Swiss or American cheese and add a slice of ham. Spread ham with French-style mustard or mayonnaise according to preference.

3. Complete the sandwich with another slice of bread and butter the outside of both sandwiches.

4. Grill the sandwiches on both sides in a skillet until the cheese melts.

5. Serve with sweet pickles.

Notes:

Avocado-Cheese Grill

Difficulty rating: EASY

Equipment needed: Skillet

Serves: 3-4

Estimated preparation time: 15-20 minutes

INGREDIENTS

6-8 slices bacon

2 large bread rolls

1 avocado

1½ cups grated Swiss or Cheddar cheese

blue cheese dressing

BASIC STEPS

1. Fry 6-8 slices bacon until crisp. Drain on a paper towel and set aside.

2. Split 2 large bread rolls and toast. Butter the top side of each roll.

3. Peel and slice 1 avocado into thin pieces.

4. Cover rolls with a layer of avocado slices and sprinkle with a generous amount (about 1½ cups) of grated Swiss or Cheddar cheese.

5. Place under broiler until cheese melts. Top with bacon strips and a spoonful of blue cheese dressing.

Notes:

Sloppy Joes

Difficulty rating: EASY

Equipment needed: Skillet

Serves: 6-8

Estimated preparation time:
20-25 minutes

INGREDIENTS

½ cup onions
½ cup green peppers
½ cup mushrooms

2 tablespoons butter or
   margarine

1 pound ground beef
½ pound ground sausage

⅓ cup chili sauce or catsup
   salt and pepper

6-8 hamburger buns

BASIC STEPS

1. Finely chop ½ cup onions, ½ cup green peppers and ½ cup mushrooms.

2. Heat 2 tablespoons butter or margarine in a skillet and saute onions and peppers 5 minutes.

3. Blend in 1 pound ground beef and ½ pound ground sausage and cook until meat is no longer red.

4. Add in the mushrooms and ⅓ cup chili sauce or catsup. Salt and pepper to taste. Let simmer for 8-10 minutes.

5. Serve on toasted hamburger buns.

Notes:

English Muffin Pizza

Difficulty rating: VERY EASY

Equipment needed: None

Serves: Variable-about 2 muffin halves per person

Estimated preparation time: 15-20 minutes

INGREDIENTS	BASIC STEPS
English muffins	1. Split and toast desired number of English muffins.
butter or margarine pizza or spaghetti sauce	2. Spread cut sides of muffins with butter or margarine. Cover each muffin half with 2 tablespoons of your favorite pizza or spaghetti sauce. Or, refer to page 194 for instructions on how to make your own.
Mozzarella cheese	3. Blanket the sauce with a piece of Mozzarella cheese.
	4. Place under broiler about 3-4 inches from heat source and cook until cheese has melted (about 4-5 minutes).

Notes:

French Bread Pizza

Difficulty rating: VERY EASY

Equipment needed: Baking sheet

Serves: Variable

Estimated preparation time: 15-20 minutes

INGREDIENTS

1 loaf French bread

pizza or spaghetti sauce

½ pound sliced Mozzarella cheese

BASIC STEPS

1. Preheat oven at 450⁰.

2. Cut 1 loaf of French bread in half lengthwise.

3. Spread the cut side of bread with a layer of your favorite prepared pizza or spaghetti sauce. Or, refer to page 194 for instructions on how to prepare your own.

4. Cover the sauce with a layer of sliced Mozzarella cheese and add one or two of your favorite toppings if you like.

5. Place on a baking sheet and bake for 10-12 minutes until cheese begins to melt.

Notes:

Shopping Tips

- Always use a shopping list.
- Keep a pad and pen close at hand so you can make a running list of what you will need the next time you go to the store.
- Keep a record of food expenditures.
- Check newspaper ads for bargain prices and weekly specials.
- Take advantage of coupons. Used judiciously, they can save you a noticeable amount of money on food bills.
- Take the time to use unit pricing.
- Begin to educate yourself to the best seasonal buys. The most obvious example is the purchase of produce when it's in season.
- Take advantage of your store's (e.g., A&P, Giant, Safeway, etc.) brand products. When compared to national brands, prices are lower and the quality is about the same.
- Avoid convenience products. Remember, the more a manufacturer has to do to the product the more it will cost you.
- It's generally a good idea to plan only one or two trips to the store each week. This will save you a lot of time, not to mention transportation costs.
- In general it's wise to shop alone (i.e., without children) and *after* you've eaten.
- Keep your receipts and don't be hesitant to return damaged or spoiled goods.

Entrees

Leg Of Lamb With Mint Jelly

Difficulty rating: VERY EASY

Equipment needed: Roasting pan

Serves: 6-8

Estimated preparation time: 2 hours

INGREDIENTS

4 pound leg of lamb
2 tablespoons vegetable oil

4 sprigs rosemary
4 thin strips of lemon rind
   salt and pepper

1 jar mint jelly

BASIC STEPS

1. Preheat oven at 400°.

2. Rub a 4 pound leg of lamb with 2 tablespoons vegetable oil.

3. Cut 8 incisions in the lamb and alternate 4 springs of rosemary and 4 thin strips of lemon rind. Sprinkle with salt and pepper.

4. Roast the lamb at 400° for 20 minutes and then reduce to 325° for another 1½ hours.

5. Slice and serve with mint jelly.

Notes:

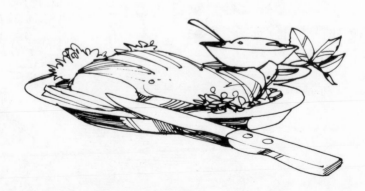

Gingered Lamb Chops

Difficulty rating: VERY EASY

Serves: 4

Equipment needed: Bowl, three-quart baking dish, rack and broiler pan & grater

Estimated preparation time: 15-20 minutes

INGREDIENTS

½ cup vegetable oil
⅓ cup lemon juice
2 tablespoons honey
1 teaspoon ginger
1 tablespoon grated lemon rind
  salt and pepper

8 lamb chops

BASIC STEPS

1. In a bowl, combine ½ cup vegetable oil, ⅓ cup lemon juice, 2 tablespoons honey, 1 teaspoon ginger and 1 tablespoon grated lemon rind. Salt and pepper to taste. Mix well.

2. Place 8 lamb chops in a shallow casserole dish and cover with the sauce. Marinate for 3-4 hours.

3. Remove chops and arrange on a rack in a broiler pan. Broil 6-8 minutes on each side. Baste occasionally with marinade.

4. Serve immediately.

Notes:

Kitchen Tips
If you ever oversweeten a recipe, add a few drops of vinegar or a pinch of salt.

Sautéed Frogs' Legs

Difficulty rating: EASY

Equipment needed: Skillet & bowl

Serves: 3-4

Estimated preparation time: 20-25 minutes

INGREDIENTS

12 pairs frozen frogs' legs

4 eggs
1 tablespoon finely chopped onion

2 cups prepared bread crumbs

3 tablespoons butter

lemon wedges
tartar sauce
parsley

BASIC STEPS

1. Thaw 12 pairs of frozen frogs' legs. Wash and dry with a towel.

2. In a bowl, beat 4 eggs. Also finely chop 1 tablespoon onion.

3. Place 2 cups prepared bread crumbs in a bowl.

4. Dip the frogs' legs in the eggs and then coat with the bread crumbs. Place on waxed paper.

5. Heat 3 tablespoons butter in a skillet and add in the onion. Saute the frogs' legs about 7-8 minutes on each side.

6. Serve with lemon wedges and/or tartar sauce. Garnish with a sprig of fresh parsely.

Notes:

Veal Scaloppini

Difficulty rating: EASY

Equipment needed: Skillet

Serves: 4

Estimated preparation time:
35-40 minutes

INGREDIENTS

2   pounds veal
     flour
     salt and pepper

½   cup mushrooms
1   green pepper

2   tablespoons butter

1   tablespoon butter

½   cup Marsala wine
1   chicken bouillon cube

BASIC STEPS

1. Cut 2 pounds of thinly sliced veal into 4-5 inch squares. Cover lightly with all-purpose flour. Salt and pepper to taste. Set aside.

2. Slice ½ cup mushrooms and cut 1 green pepper into thin strips.

3. Heat 2 tablespoons butter in a skillet and saute green peppers 3-4 minutes. Add in mushrooms and cook another 3 minutes. Remove vegetables and set aside.

4. Add another tablespoon of butter and saute veal squares until nicely brown on both sides. Remove from heat and drain butter from skillet.

5. Return to heat and blend in ½ cup Marsala wine and ½ cup chicken bouillon.

6. Simmer for 5-6 minutes. Add in the vegetables, simmer for another 2-3 minutes and serve hot.

Notes:

French Style Veal

Difficulty rating: VERY EASY

Equipment needed: Skillet

Serves: 4

Estimated preparation time:
20 minutes

INGREDIENTS

2 pounds veal

1 cup mushrooms

⅓ cup all-purpose flour

2 eggs

2 tablespoons butter

BASIC STEPS

1. Cut 2 pounds of thinly sliced veal into 4-5 inch squares.

2. Slice 1 cup mushrooms.

3. Place ⅓ cup all-purpose flour in a bowl.

4. Beat 2 eggs.

5. Coat each slice of veal with flour and dip in the eggs.

6. Heat 2 tablespoons butter in a skillet and saute veal for 5 minutes on each side. Drain and keep warm.

7. Saute the mushrooms in the remaining butter for 3-4 minutes.

8. Serve veal with the mushrooms.

Notes:

Quiche Lorraine

Difficulty rating: EASY

Equipment needed: Pie or quiche dish, skillet & mixing bowl

Serves: 4-6

Estimated preparation time: 60-75 minutes

INGREDIENTS

1 9-inch pie shell

1 cup shredded Swiss cheese

6 strips bacon or
½ cup diced ham

1½ cups whipping cream
3 eggs
¼ teaspoon nutmeg
¼ teaspoon Worcestershire sauce
pepper

BASIC STEPS

1. Preheat oven at 425°.

2. Make ready an uncooked 9-inch pie crust. You can buy ready-made frozen shells at your local supermarket or refer to page 197 for instructions on how to make your own.

3. Shred or cut into small cubes 1 cup of Swiss cheese. Spread over the bottom of pie crust.

4. Fry 6 strips of bacon until crisp or cut ½ cup of cooked ham into bite size pieces. Sprinkle over Swiss cheese.

5. In a bowl, combine 1½ cups whipping cream, 3 eggs, ¼ teaspoon nutmeg, ¼ teaspoon Worcestershire sauce and a dash of pepper. Mix well.

6. Pour over the ingredients in pie shell.

7. Bake at 425° for 15 minutes and then reduce heat to 325° and bake for another 35-40 minutes.

8. Remove from oven and let stand for 20 minutes before serving.

Notes:

Spinach Quiche

Difficulty rating: EASY

Equipment needed: Pie or quiche dish, one-quart saucepan, mixing bowl & grater

Serves: 4-6

Estimated preparation time: 60-75 minutes

INGREDIENTS

1 9-inch pie shell

1 cup shredded Swiss cheese

1 package (10 ounces) chopped spinach

1½ cups whipping cream
3 eggs
¼ teaspoon nutmeg
¼ teaspoon Worcestershire sauce
pepper

BASIC STEPS

1. Preheat oven at 425º.

2. Make ready an uncooked 9-inch pie crust. You can buy ready-made frozen shells at your local supermarket or refer to page 197 for instructions on how to make your own.

3. Shred or cut into small cubes 1 cup of Swiss cheese. Spread over bottom of pie crust.

4. Cook a package (10 ounces) of frozen spinach according to directions. Drain.

5. Combine in a bowl, 1½ cups whipping cream, 3 eggs, ¼ teaspoon nutmeg, ¼ teaspoon Worcestershire sauce and a dash of pepper. Gently mix in chopped spinach.

6. Pour over the ingredients in pie shell.

7. Bake at 425º for 15 minutes and then reduce heat to 325º and bake for another 35-40 minutes.

8. Remove from oven and let stand for 20 minutes before serving.

Notes:

Fettuccine Alfredo

Difficutly rating: EASY

Serves: 2-3

Equipment needed: Large kettle, 2 bowls & colander

Estimated preparation time: 20-25 minutes

INGREDIENTS

¼ cup sour cream
¼ cup whipping cream

8 ounces fettuccine

1 stick (¼ pound) butter
salt and pepper

3 tablespoons grated Parmesan cheese

grated Parmesan
nutmeg

BASIC STEPS

1. In a bowl, mix together ¼ cup sour cream and ¼ cup whipping cream. Set aside.

2. Cook about 8 ounces of fettuccine according to directions on package. Drain in colander.

3. Transfer to a large bowl and toss with 1 stick (¼ pound) butter cut into smaller pieces. Salt and pepper to taste.

4. Pour on cream mixture and mix until evenly distributed.

5. Add 3 tablespoons grated Parmesan cheese and toss again.

6. Divide into appropriate number of portions and serve with a sprinkling of grated Parmesan cheese and a light touch of nutmeg.

Notes:

Kitchen Tips ✓
To keep the water from boiling over when cooking rice and pasta, add a tablespoon of oil or butter.

Spinach Fettuccine

Difficulty rating: EASY

Equipment needed: Mixing bowl & kettle

Serves: 3-4

Estimated preparation time: 25-30 minutes

INGREDIENTS	BASIC STEPS
¼ cup sour cream ¼ cup whipping cream	1. In a bowl, mix together ¼ cup sour cream and ¼ cup whipping cream. Set aside.
8 ounces fettuccine	2. Cook 8 ounces of fettuccine according to package directions. Drain in a colander.
1 package (10 ounces) frozen chopped spinach	3. While the fettuccine is cooking prepare 1 package (10 ounces) frozen chopped spinach according to package directions. Drain.
¼ pound butter salt and pepper	4. Transfer fettuccine to a large bowl and toss with 1 stick (¼ pound) butter cut into smaller pieces. Salt and pepper to taste.
	5. Pour cream mixture over fettuccine and blend in the spinach.
¼ cup grated Parmesan cheese	6. Add ¼ cup grated Parmesan cheese and toss until noodles are evenly covered.
¼ cup grated Parmesan cheese	7. Serve with a sprinkling of Parmesan cheese.

Notes:

Manicotti

Difficulty rating: EASY

Equipment needed: Saucepan, three-quart baking dish & mixing bowl

Serves: 2-3

Estimated preparation time: 70-80 minutes

INGREDIENTS

1 cup ricotta cheese
1 tablespoon grated Parmesan cheese
1 egg
  salt and pepper

1 pint tomato sauce

6-7 manicotti shells

  grated Parmesan cheese

BASIC STEPS

1. In a bowl, combine 1 cup ricotta cheese, 1 tablespoon grated Parmesan cheese, and 1 well beaten egg. Salt and pepper to taste.

2. Make ready 1 pint tomato sauce. You can open a jar of your favorite ready-made sauce or prepare your own by following the recipe on page 193 (without meat) or page 194 (with meat).

3. Cook 6-7 manicotti shells according to directions on package.

4. Stuff each shell with cheese mixture and arrange in a shallow baking dish.

5. Pour tomato sauce over shells and sprinkle with grated Parmesan cheese. Bake at 350° for 50-60 minutes.

Notes:

Kitchen Tips ✓
Because most of the sauces or foods that accompany pasta are already salted, it is usually unnecessary to add salt to the water in which it is cooked.

Baked Fettuccine

Difficulty rating: EASY

Equipment needed: Colander, three-quart baking dish & mixing bowl

Serves: 4-6

Estimated preparation time: 40-50 minutes

INGREDIENTS

1 pound fettuccine noodles

2 sticks (½ pound) butter

4 eggs
⅓ cup whipping cream
⅓ cup sour cream

¾ cup grated Romano cheese

Italian seasoned bread crumbs

BASIC STEPS

1. Preheat oven at 300º.

2. Cook 1 pound fettuccine noodles according to directions on package. Drain in a colander and return to original cooking pan.

3. Blend in 2 sticks (½ pound) butter until noodles are evenly coated.

4. In a separate bowl, beat together 4 eggs and add in ⅓ cup whipping cream and ⅓ cup sour cream. Pour over the noodles and mix thoroughly.

5. Spread ¾ cup grated Romano cheese over noodles and toss well.

6. Transfer noodles to shallow baking dish and top with a sprinkling of Italian seasoned bread crumbs.

7. Bake for 20-25 minutes.

Notes:

Noodle Casserole

Difficulty rating: EASY

Equipment needed: Skillet, two-quart casserole dish & grater

Serves: 4-6

Estimated preparation time: 65-75 minutes

INGREDIENTS

8 ounces noodles

1 onion
1 green pepper
1 clove of garlic
1 cup sliced mushrooms

2-3 tablespoons butter or margarine
1 pound ground beef

2 cans (15 ounces each) tomato sauce
1 teaspoon salt
¼ teaspoon pepper
½ teaspoon basil
½ teaspoon oregano

½ pound grated cheddar cheese

BASIC STEPS

1. Preheat oven at 325°.

2. Prepare 8 ounces of noodles according to directions on package. Drain in a colander and set aside.

3. Chop 1 onion, 1 green pepper, 1 clove of garlic and slice 1 cup of mushrooms.

4. Heat 2-3 tablespoons butter or margarine in a skillet and saute onions, peppers and garlic. Add in one pound ground beef and the mushrooms and cook unitl meat is no longer red.

5. Blend in 2 cans (15 ounces each) tomato sauce and flavor with 1 teaspoon salt, ¼ teaspoon pepper, ½ teaspoon basil and ½ teaspoon oregano.

6. In a casserole dish, combine the noodles and meat sauce and mix thoroughly.

7. Cover with ½ pound grated cheddar cheese and bake for 40-45 minutes.

Notes:

97

Macaroni and Cheese

Difficulty rating: EASY

Equiment needed: Blender, kettle & two-quart casserole dish

Serves: 4-5

Estimated preparation time: 70-80 minutes

INGREDIENTS

2 cups macaroni

¾ cup milk
2 eggs
¼ cup sour cream

1 cup grated cheddar cheese

bread crumbs

BASIC STEPS

1. Measure out 2 cups of macaroni and drop into a kettle containing 2 quarts of boiling salted water. Boil about 20 minutes or follow directions on package. Drain well in colander. Return to original cooking pan.

2. In a separate bowl, combine ¾ cup milk, 2 eggs and ¼ cup sour cream. Mix well.

3. Add contents of this bowl to the pan of macaroni. Mix in ¾ cup grated cheddar cheese (save ¼ cup until later) until ingredients are evely combined.

4. Transfer this mixture to a greased casserole dish and top off with the remaining ¼ cup of cheddar and a sprinkling of bread crumbs.

5. Bake at 375° in a pan of hot water for 45 minutes.

Notes:

Linguine With Clam Sauce

Difficulty rating: EASY

Serves: 4-6

Equipment needed: Skillet & kettle

Estimated preparation time: 30-40 minutes

INGREDIENTS	BASIC STEPS
½ cup scallions	1. Chop ½ cup scallions using a portion of green tops.
2 tablespoons margarine or butter	2. Heat 2 tablespoons of margarine or butter in a large skillet and saute scallions for 2-3 minutes.
½ cup vegetable oil 2 cloves garlic 1 can (8 ounces) minced clams salt and pepper	3. Add in ½ cup vegetable oil, 2 finely chopped cloves of garlic and 1 can of minced clams. Salt and pepper to taste and simmer.
1 package linguine (16 ounces)	4. Cook a 16 ounce package of linguine according to directions. Drain in a colander and return to original cooking pan.
	5. Add the clam sauce to the linguine and mix thoroughly.
¼ cup grated Parmesan cheese	6. Serve with a sprinkling of grated Parmesan cheese.

Notes:

Kitchen Tips✔
In cooking pasta you should use three units of water to one of pasta.

Eggplant Parmigiana

Difficulty rating: EASY

Equipment needed: Skillet, mixing bowl & three-quart baking dish

Serves: 4

Estimated preparation time: 45-55 minutes

INGREDIENTS

1 eggplant

2 eggs

1 cup bread crumbs
2 teaspoons oregano
1 teaspoon basil

2 tablespoons butter or margarine

1½-2 cups tomato sauce

½ cup grated Parmesan
½ pound sliced Mozzarella cheese

BASIC STEPS

1. Preheat oven at 350º.

2. Pare 1 eggplant and cut into slices about ¼ inch thick.

3. In a bowl, beat 2 eggs.

4. Combine in a separate bowl, 1 cup bread crumbs with 2 teaspoons oregano and 1 teaspoon basil. Mix thoroughly.

5. Dip each slice of eggplant in the eggs and then cover with bread crumbs.

6. Heat 2 tablespoons butter of margarine in a skillet and saute both sides of the eggplant until nicely browned.

7. Arrange eggplant slices on the bottom of a shallow casserole dish and cover with a layer of your favorite tomato sauce. Or, 194 for instructions on how to make your own.

8. Cover with a generous sprinkling of grated Parmesan cheese and top with a single layer of Mozzarella cheese.

9. Bake for 25-30 minutes.

Notes:

Ratatouille

Difficulty rating: EASY

Equipment needed: Large skillet

Serves: 3-4

Estimated preparation time:
25-30 minutes

INGREDIENTS

1 eggplant
2 onions
2 tomatoes
1 green pepper
1 zucchini
2 cloves garlic

½ cup olive oil
½ teaspoon oregano
½ teaspoon basil
salt and pepper

BASIC STEPS

1. Cut 1 eggplant into bite size cubes, chop 2 onions, and peel and quarter 2 tomatoes. Slice 1 green pepper and 1 zucchini and finely chop 2 cloves of garlic.

2. Heat ½ cup olive oil in a large skillet and saute onions and garlic for about 5 minutes. Add the other vegetables and season with ½ teaspoon oregano and ½ teaspoon basil. Salt and pepper to taste.

3. Cover and let simmer for 10-15 minutes.*

*Note: Adjust cooking time according to how you like your vegetables. Ten to fifteen minutes cooking time allows vegetable to retain their crispness.

Notes:

Curried Mushrooms On Muffins

Difficulty rating: VERY EASY

Equipment needed: Skillet

Serves: 4

Estimated preparation time:
15-20 minutes

INGREDIENTS

1 pound mushrooms

2 tablespoons butter or
margarine

⅓ cup cooking sherry
1 cup sour cream
1 tablespoon curry powder
salt and pepper

2-4 English muffins

BASIC STEPS

1. Slice 1 pound of mushrooms.

2. Heat 2 tablespoons butter or
margarine in a skillet and saute
mushrooms for 2-3 minutes.

3. Blend in ⅓ cup cooking sherry,
1 cup sour cream and 1
tablespoon curry powder. Season
to taste with salt and pepper and
gradually add more curry
powder if you like.

4. Serve over English muffin
halves, toasted or plain. Use 1 or
2 halves to a serving.

Notes:

Cheese and Onion Casserole

Difficulty rating: EASY

Equipment needed: Two-quart
casserole dish & grater

Serves: 4

Estimated preparation time:
   1½ hours, 75-80 minutes of which
   is baking time

INGREDIENTS

1 pound potatoes
2 onions
2 cups cheddar cheese

2 eggs
⅔ cup milk
   salt and pepper

BASIC STEPS

1. Cut into thin slices, 1 pound
   potatoes and 2 onions. Also,
   grate 2 cups cheddar cheese.

2. Line the bottom of a 2-quart
   casserole dish with a layer of
   potatoes and cover with a layer of
   onions. Top with a sprinkling of
   cheese and repeat cycle ending
   with potatoes on top.

3. In a separate bowl, beat together
   2 eggs and combine with ⅔ cup
   milk. Pour over the ingredients
   in casserole. Salt and pepper to
   taste and top with pieces of butter. Bake at 350° for 75-80
   minutes.

Notes:

Tamale Pie

Difficulty rating: EASY

Equipment needed: Skillet, three-quart baking dish & grater

Serves: 6-8

Estimated preparation time:
70-80 minutes, approximately 40-50 minutes of which is baking time

INGREDIENTS

1 onion
1 green pepper
½ cup black olives
1 cup cheddar cheese

2 tablespoons vegetable oil

1 pound ground beef
½ pound ground sausage

2 cans (16 ounces each) tomatoes
1 can (12 ounces) whole kernel corn (drained)
¾ cup corn meal
1½ teaspoons chili powder
salt and pepper

BASIC STEPS

1. Chop 1 onion and 1 green pepper. Also shred 1 cup cheddar cheese and chop ½ cup black olives and set aside.

2. Heat 2 tablespoons vegetable oil in a skillet and saute onions and peppers 5 minutes.

3. Add 1 pound ground beef and ½ pound ground sausage and cook until meat is no longer red.

4. Blend in 2 cans (16 ounces each) tomatoes, 1 can (12 ounces drained) whole kernel corn, ¾ cup corn meal, 1½ teaspoons chili powder and add ½ cup chopped black olives. Mix well and salt and pepper to taste.

5. Transfer the contents of the skillet to a large baking dish and top with 1 cup shredded cheddar cheese.

6. Bake at 350° for 40-50 minutes.

Notes:

Italian Casserole

Difficulty rating: EASY

Equipment needed: Skillet &
three-quart baking dish

Serves: 6-8

Estimated preparation time:
70-80 minutes

INGREDIENTS	BASIC STEPS
	1. Preheat oven at 350°.
2 cups mushrooms	2. Slice 2 cups mushrooms.
8 ounces noodles	3. Cook 8 ounces noodles according to directions on package. Drain and set aside.
1 pound ground hot sausage	4. In a skillet, brown 1 pound hot sausage. Add in mushrooms and cook another 3-5 minutes.
32 ounces spaghetti sauce ½ teaspoon oregano ¼ teaspoon basil salt and pepper	5. Blend in 32 ounces of your favorite prepared spaghetti sauce to the skillet mixture. Or, refer to page 194 for instructions on how to prepare your own. Also, add in the noodles, ½ teaspoon oregano and ¼ teaspoon basil. Salt and pepper to taste.
1 pound Ricotta cheese	6. Transfer half of this mixture to a shallow baking dish. Blanket this layer with 1 pound Ricotta cheese and pour the remaining contents of the skillet over the cheese.
¼ cup grated Romano cheese	7. Top with ¼ cup grated Romano cheese and bake for 40-50 minutes.

Notes:

Cheese and Rice Casserole

Difficulty rating: EASY

Equipment needed: Two-quart casserole dish, skillet & saucepan

Serves: 4-6

Estimated preparation time:
80-90 minutes, approximately 60 minutes of which is baking time

INGREDIENTS

2 cups uncooked rice

1 cup celery
6-8 scallions

2-3 tablespoons butter or margarine

2 eggs
¼ cup vegetable oil
1 cup milk
1 cup grated cheddar cheese
1 cup Roquefort cheese
salt and pepper

BASIC STEPS

1. Measure out 2 cups uncooked rice and prepare according to directions on package. Or, refer to page 192 for instructions on how to cook rice.

2. While rice is cooking, chop 1 cup celery and 6-8 scallions.

3. Heat 2-3 tablespoons butter or margarine in a skillet and saute celery and scallions for 5-6 minutes. Drain and set aside.

4. When rice is finished cooking, transfer to a large mixing bowl and combine rice with the celery and scallions and add in 2 well beaten eggs, ¼ cup vegetable oil, 1 cup milk, 1 cup grated cheddar cheese and 1 cup crumbled Roquefort cheese. Salt and Pepper to taste.

5. Transfer to a casserole dish and bake at 350º for 60 minutes.

Notes:

Cheese Bake

Difficulty rating: EASY

Serves: 3-4

Equipment needed: Two-quart casserole dish, saucepan & bowl

Estimated preparation time: 50-60 minutes

INGREDIENTS

2 cups bread crumbs

2-3 tablespoons butter or margarine
2 cups milk

1 cup cheddar cheese
½ cup Roquefort cheese

3 eggs
½ teaspoon salt
¼ teaspoon Tabasco sauce
1 teaspoon Worcestershire sauce

¼ cup grated Romano cheese

BASIC STEPS

1. Preheat oven at 400°.

2. Prepare 2 cups bread crumbs.

3. In a saucepan, melt 2-3 tablespoons butter or margarine and add in 2 cups milk. Let simmer for 3-5 minutes.

4. Pour the milk over the bread crumbs and let stand for 10 minutes.

5. While the bread crumbs are soaking grate 1 cup cheddar cheese and crumble ½ cup Roquefort cheese.

6. In a separate bowl, beat 3 eggs and add in the cheeses, ½ teaspoon salt, ¼ teaspoon Tabasco sauce and 1 teaspoon Worcestershire sauce.

7. Combine with the milk and bread crumbs mixture and mix well.

8. Transfer to a casserole dish and sprinkle with ¼ cup grated Romano cheese.

9. Bake for 30-35 minutes.

Notes:

Eggplant-Tomato Casserole

Difficulty rating: EASY

Equipment needed: Skillet &
casserole dish

Serves: 4-6

Estimated preparation time:
  60-75 minutes

INGREDIENTS

1 eggplant
½ cup onions

3 tablespoons butter or
  margarine

1½ cans (16 ounces each)
  tomatoes
1 tablespoon parsley
½ teaspoon thyme
1 teaspoon salt
⅛ teaspoon pepper

1 cup grated cheddar cheese
1 cup croutons

BASIC STEPS

1. Preheat oven at 350º.

2. Cut 1 eggplant into bite size
   pieces and chop ½ cup onions.

3. Heat 3 tablespoons butter or
   margarine in a skillet and saute
   eggplant for 5-6 minutes. Add in
   onions and saute another 3-4
   minutes.

4. Blend in 1½ cans (16 ounces
   each) tomatoes, 1 tablespoon
   parsley, ½ teaspoon thyme, 1
   teaspoon salt and ⅛ teaspoon
   pepper.

5. Transfer to casserole dish and
   top with 1 cup grated cheddar
   cheese and 1 cup croutons. Bake
   for 40-50 minutes.

Notes:

Cheese-Nut Casserole

Difficulty rating: EASY

Equipment needed: Bowl, two-quart casserole dish & grater

Serves: 4-6

Estimated preparation time: 35-45 minutes

INGREDIENTS

1 cup English walnuts
1 cup cheddar cheese
½ cup Roquefort cheese

2 cups bread crumbs
1 cup milk
1 egg
½ teaspoon salt
⅛ teaspoon pepper
½ teaspoon basil
1 tablespoon parsley
1 teaspoon Worcestershire sauce

BASIC STEPS

1. Preheat oven at 350°.

2. Chop 1 cup English walnuts and grate 1 cup cheddar cheese. Also, crumble ½ cup Roquefort cheese.

3. In a bowl, combine 2 cups bread crumbs and 1 cup milk. Add in 1 well beaten egg, ½ teaspoon salt, ⅛ teaspoon pepper, ½ teaspoon basil, 1 tablespoon parsley and 1 teaspoon Worcestershire sauce.

4. Blend in the walnuts and cheeses and mix thoroughly.

5. Transfer to a casserole dish and bake for 25-30 minutes.

Notes:

Hamburger and Corn Casserole

Difficulty rating: EASY

Equipment needed: Skillet, two-quart casserole dish & bowl

Serves: 4-6

Estimated preparation time:
60 minutes, approximately half of which is baking time

INGREDIENTS

1 onion
2 green peppers
2 tomatoes

2 packages (10 ounces each) frozen whole kernel corn

2-3 tablespoons butter or margarine
1 pound ground beef

2 eggs
salt and pepper

½ cup bread crumbs

BASIC STEPS

1. Preheat oven at 375º.

2. Chop 1 onion and 2 green peppers. Also, slice 2 tomatoes.

3. Cook 2 packages (10 ounces each) frozen whole kernel corn according to directions on package. Drain and set aside.

4. Heat 2-3 tablespoons butter or margarine in a skillet and saute the onions and peppers for 5-6 minutes. Add in 1 pound ground beef and cook until meat is no longer red. Salt and pepper to taste.

5. In a bowl, beat 2 eggs and mix thoroughly with the corn. Salt and pepper to taste.

6. Grease a casserole dish and pour the corn mixture on the bottom and cover with ½ of the meat mixture. Insert a layer of tomatoes and repeat cycle with remaining ingredients. Top with ½ cup bread crumbs.

7. Bake for 35-40 minutes.

Notes:

Baked Beans

Difficulty rating: VERY EASY

Equipment needed: Two-quart bean pot or casserole, bowl & colander

Serves: 6-8

Estimated preparation time: 4½ to 5 hours, approximately 4 hours of which is baking time

INGREDIENTS

1 pound navy beans
3 cups water

1 teaspoon salt
2 cups water

¾ cup brown sugar
¼ cup molasses
¼ pound butter
1 cup catsup
1 can (6 ounces) tomato sauce
1 teaspoon dry mustard

½ pound bacon

BASIC STEPS

1. Soak 1 pound navy beans in a kettle overnight in 3 cups water.

2. Add 1 teaspoon salt and 2 cups water to the beans. Bring to a boil, reduce heat, and simmer for 60 minutes.

3. Drain the beans in a colander and transfer to a 2-quart bean pot or casserole.

4. In a separate bowl, mix together ¾ cup brown sugar, ¼ cup molasses, ¼ pound butter, 1 cup catsup, 1 can (6 ounces) tomato sauce and 1 teaspoon dry mustard.

5. Pour this mixture over beans and stir.

6. Mix in ½ pound bacon strips and bake at 325⁰ for about 4 hours until beans are tender.

Notes:

Tortilla Bake

Difficulty rating: EASY

Serves: 4-6

Equipment needed: Skillet & two-quart casserole dish

Estimated preparation time: 40-50 minutes

INGREDIENTS

1 onion
1 green pepper

2 tablespoons butter or margarine
1 pound ground beef
½ pound ground sausage

1 can (15 ounces) tomato sauce
1 can (12 ounces) whole kernel corn (drained)
2 tablespoons chili powder
salt and pepper

½ pound grated cheddar cheese
1 package (9 ounces) frozen tortillas

olives (green or black)

BASIC STEPS

1. Preheat oven at 325°.

2. Chop 1 onion and 1 green pepper.

3. Heat 2 tablespoons butter or margarine in a skillet and saute onions and peppers 5 minutes. Add in 1 pound ground beef and ½ pound ground sausage and cook until meat is no longer red.

4. Mix in 1 can (15 ounces) tomato sauce, 1 can (12 ounces) whole kernel corn (drained) and 2 tablespoons chili powder. Salt and pepper to taste and let simmer for 5-7 minutes.

5. Grate ½ pound cheddar cheese and open 1 package (9 ounces) frozen tortillas.

6. Arrange half of the tortillas on the bottom of a 2-quart casserole dish and blanket with a layer of the meat sauce. Top the meat sauce with a layer of cheese and repeat cycle.

7. Top with a sprinkling of olives (green or black) and bake for 25-30 minutes.

Notes:

Cheese-Zucchini Casserole

Difficulty rating: EASY

Equipment needed: Skillet, three-quart baking dish & mixing bowl

Serves: 4-5

Estimated preparation time: 60-70 minutes

INGREDIENTS

¼ cup whole wheat flour
½ teaspoon salt
½ teaspoon oregano
⅛ teaspoon pepper
¼ teaspoon garlic powder

2 zucchini

3 tablespoons vegetable oil

½ pound sliced provolone cheese

2 tomatoes

1 cup sour cream
1 teaspoon salt
1 teaspoon oregano
¼ teaspoon pepper
¼ teaspoon garlic powder
½ cup grated Parmesan cheese

BASIC STEPS

1. Preheat oven at 350⁰.

2. In a bowl, combine ¼ cup whole wheat flour, ½ teaspoon salt, ½ teaspoon oregano, ⅛ teaspoon pepper and ¼ teaspoon garlic powder.

3. Cut 2 zucchini into slices about ¼ inch thick.

4. Coat each slice of zucchini in flour mixture.

5. Heat 3 tablespoons vegetable oil in a skillet and cook zucchini slices until brown on both sides.

6. Drain, and arrange slices on the bottom of a shallow baking dish that has been oiled.

7. Cover the zucchini with a layer of sliced provolone cheese (about ½ pound).

8. Add a layer of sliced tomatoes (about 2 tomatoes) to the cheese.

9. Mix together in a separate bowl, 1 cup sour cream, 1 teaspoon salt, 1 teaspoon oregano, ¼ teaspoon pepper and ¼ teaspoon garlic powder and pour over other ingredients in casserole. Top with ½ cup Parmesan cheese.

10. Bake for 30 minutes.

Hamburger Casserole

Difficulty rating: VERY EASY

Equipment needed: Skillet & two-quart casserole dish

Serves: 4-5

Estimated preparation time:
70-80 minutes, approximately 60 minutes of which is baking time.

INGREDIENTS

1 cup green peppers
1 cup onions
1 cup mushrooms

2 tablespoons vegetable oil

1 pound ground beef

1 can (16 ounces) tomatoes
½ cup uncooked rice
½ cup water

½ teaspoon thyme
¼ teaspoon garlic powder
salt and pepper

BASIC STEPS

1. Chop 1 cup green peppers, 1 cup onions and 1 cup mushrooms.

2. In a large skillet, heat 2 tablespoons vegetable oil and saute onions and peppers 5 minutes. Add mushrooms and cook another 3-5 minutes.

3. Add 1 pound ground beef and cook unitl meat is no longer red.

4 Mix in 1 can (16 ounces) tomatoes (including juice), ½ cup uncooked rice and ½ cup water.

5. Flavor with ½ teaspoon thyme, ¼ teaspoon garlic powder and salt and pepper to taste.

6. Transfer to a casserole dish and bake at 350º for 1 hour.

Notes:

Cabbage Casserole

Difficulty rating: EASY

Equipment needed: Grater, two-quart casserole dish & saucepan

Serves: 4-6

Estimated preparation time: 50-60 minutes

INGREDIENTS

1 head cabbage

1 cup milk
1 cup sour cream
1½ cups grated cheddar cheese
½ teaspoon salt
⅛ teaspoon pepper
½ teaspoon paprika

1 cup bread crumbs

BASIC STEPS

1. Preheat oven at 325º.

2. Shred 1 head cabbage and cook in boiling water for 7 minutes. Drain in a colander and set aside.

3. In a bowl, mix together 1 cup milk, 1 cup sour cream, 1½ cups grated cheddar cheese, ½ teaspoon salt, ⅛ teaspoon pepper and ½ teaspoon paprika.

4. Add the cabbage to the sour cream and cheese mixture and stir gently.

5. Transfer to a greased casserole dish and top with 1 cup bread crumbs. Bake for 30-40 minutes.

Notes:

Broiled Fish Fillets With Curry

Difficulty rating: VERY EASY

Serves: 1-2

Equipment needed: Shallow broiling pan

Estimated preparation time: 15-20 minutes

INGREDIENTS

1½ pounds fish fillets
(turbot, flounder or sole)

butter
lemon salt
ginger
curry powder

BASIC STEPS

1. Arrange 1-1½ pounds of fish fillets (turbot, flounder or sole) on a shallow broiling pan.

2. Sprinkle fillets with a few chunks of butter or margarine, some lemon salt, ginger and curry powder.

3. Place under broiler about 4 inches from heat source and cook fish without turning until it flakes (about 8-10 minutes).

4. Serve with lemon wedges.

Notes:

Kitchen Tips
A few pieces of dried bread in a broiler pan will readily absorb dripping fat and prevent oven fires.

Scalloped Oysters

Difficulty rating: VERY EASY

Equipment needed: Two-quart casserole dish

Serves: 4

Estimated preparation time: 40-45 minutes

INGREDIENTS	BASIC STEPS
	1. Preheat oven at 350°.
1½ cups crackers	2. Prepare 1½ cups coarsely crumbled crackers (soda crackers or Ritz).
1 pint oysters ½ pound butter salt and pepper	3. Cover the bottom of a small casserole dish with a portion of the crackers. Top with a layer of oysters and blanket this with a few chunks of butter and a sprinkling of salt and pepper. Repeat this procedure until crackers and oysters are used up.
1½ cups half & half cream	4. Add 1½ cups half & half cream and bake for 30 minutes.

Notes:

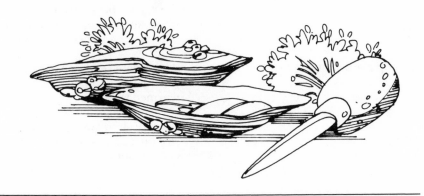

Curried Shrimp

Difficulty rating: EASY

Equipment needed: Large skillet & saucepan

Serves: 4

Estimated preparation time: 45-60 minutes

INGREDIENTS

1   onion
2   cloves of garlic

2   tablespoons vegetable oil

1   tablespoon curry powder
1   tablespoon lemon juice
1   can (16 ounces tomatoes)

rice for 4 people

1   pound uncooked shrimp

¾   cup plain yogurt

BASIC STEPS

1. Chop 1 onion and finely chop 2 cloves of garlic.

2. Heat 2 tablespoons vegetable oil in a large skillet and saute onions and garlic for about 5 minutes.

3. To this mixture add 1 tablespoon curry, 1 tablespoon lemon juice and 1 can (16 ounces) tomatoes. Cook for another 10 minutes. Taste, and, if you desire, gradually add more curry powder.

4. While this mixture is cooking, start to prepare enough rice for 4. You can use prepackaged rice and follow the manufacturer's directions or refer to page 192 for instructions on how to prepare your own.

5. To the ingredients simmering in the skillet, blend in 1 pound of uncooked shrimp and continue to cook for another 15 minutes.

6. Just before serving add in ¾ cup plain yogurt and heat until warmed through.

7. Place desired amount of cooked rice on a plate and cover with curried shrimp.

Fried Fish Marinated In Wine

Difficulty rating: EASY

Serves: 2-3

Equipment needed: Skillet & two-quart casserole dish

Estimated preparation time: 20-25 minutes

INGREDIENTS

2 pounds fish fillets
1½ cups dry white wine

1 cup all-purpose flour
2 teaspoons salt
½ teaspoon pepper
½ teaspoon dillweed

⅓-½ cup butter

BASIC STEPS

1. Marinate 2 pounds of fish (turbot, flounder or sole) in 1½ cups dry white wine for 1 hour.

2. In a separate bowl, mix together 1 cup all-purpose flour, 2 teaspoons salt, ½ teaspoon pepper and ½ teaspoon dillweed.

3. Drain the fish and cover evenly with flour mixture.

4. Melt ⅓-½ cup butter in a skillet and cook on both sides until nicely brown.

Notes:

Kitchen Tips ✓
Do a quick check for fish bones before cooking by running your finger tips over the surface of the fish. When you find one, remove with tweezers.

Flounder With Sherry Sauce

Difficulty rating: EASY

Equipment needed: Skillet,
saucepan & bowl

Serves: 3-4

Estimated preparation time:
25-30 minutes

INGREDIENTS

2 pounds flounder fillets

1 cup dry white wine
1 bay leaf

2 tablespoons butter
3 tablespoons all-purpose flour
¾ cup milk

2 egg yolks
¼ cup cooking sherry

¼ cup finely chopped parsely

BASIC STEPS

1. Cut 2 pounds of flounder fillets
   into 4-6 pieces.

2. Place fillets in a skillet and cover
   with 1 cup dry white wine. Add 1
   bay leaf.

3. Bring to a broil and let simmer
   for another 5-6 minutes.

4. While the fillets are simmering,
   melt 2 tablespoons butter in a
   saucepan and blend with 3
   tablespoons all-purpose flour.
   Remove from heat and gradually
   stir in ¾ cup milk. Return to heat
   and simmer until thick.

5. When the fillets are finished
   cooking, remove to a serving dish
   and keep warm. Retain the wine
   liquid the fish was contained in.

6. In a separate bowl, combine 2
   egg yolks and ¼ cup cooking
   sherry. Mix well.

7. To the remaining white wine in
   the skillet, add the floured
   mixture together with the sherry
   and egg combination. Mix
   thoroughly. Salt and pepper to
   taste.

8. Pour desired amount of sauce
   over fish and serve with a
   sprinkle of finely chopped
   parsely.

Poached Fish

Difficulty rating: EASY

Equipment needed: Large skillet & saucepan

Serves: 4

Estimated preparation time: 20-30 minutes

INGREDIENTS

1 cup water
2 vegetarian bouillon cubes
1 tablespoon lemon juice
1 teaspoon dill

1½ pounds fish fillets (flounder, turbot or sole)

3 tablespoons butter
2 tablespoons flour
½ cup whipping cream

4 lemon wedges

BASIC STEPS

1. Heat 1 cup water to boiling in a large skillet and dissolve 2 vegetarian bouillon cubes. Add in 1 tablespoon lemon juice and 1 teaspoon dill.

2. Reduce heat to simmer and add 1½ pounds fish fillets (flounder, turbot or sole). Cover and cook about 10 minutes until fish fillets flake easily. Remove fish and keep warm retaining the liquid in the skillet.

3. In a saucepan, melt 3 tablespoons butter and blend in 2 tablespoons flour, ½ cup whipping cream and ¾ cup of the liquid the fish was cooked in. Simmer for 5-6 minutes.

4. Serve fish with sauce and garnish with a lemon wedge.

Notes:

Chicken Breasts In Grape Sauce

Difficulty rating: EASY

Serves: 4-6

Equipment needed: Roasting pan, skillet & saucepan

Estimated preparation time:
2 hours, approximately 1¼ hours of which is roasting time

INGREDIENTS

1 can (10¾ ounces) cream of mushroom soup
1 cup sour cream
3 tablespoons all-purpose flour
1 cup dry white wine
1 cup green seedless grapes
salt and pepper

4 chicken breasts

BASIC STEPS

1. Preheat oven at 350º.

2. In a saucepan, mix together 1 can (10¾ ounces) cream of mushroom soup, 1 cup sour cream, 3 tablespoons all-purpose flour, 1 cup dry white wine and 1 cup seedless grapes. Salt and pepper to taste. Let simmer 3-4 minutes.

3. Arrange 4 chicken breasts in a roasting pan and cover with the sauce.

4. Bake for 1¼ hours. Baste occasionally.

Notes:

Kitchen Tips✓
It is more economical to buy whole chickens and cut them up yourself than it is to buy the parts.

Duckling A L'Orange

Difficulty rating: MODERATELY EASY

Serves: 2

Equipment needed: Roasting pan and rack, saucepan and grater

Estimated preparation time: 2 to 2½ hours

INGREDIENTS

1 duckling, (3-4 pounds)
1 sliced orange

¼ cup honey
2 tablespoons orange juice
1 tablespoon grated orange peel
¼ teaspoon allspice
½ teaspoon dry mustard

1½ tablespoons cornstarch
1 tablespoon orange peel
1½ cups orange juice

orange slices
parsely sprigs

BASIC STEPS

1. Wash duckling, pat dry, and rub inside cavity and outside with salt and pepper. Cut wing tips off at first joint. Slice 1 orange and place in cavity.

2 Roast on a rack breast side up at 450⁰ for 20 minutes. Reduce heat to 350⁰ and continue roasting, allowing 20-25 minutes per pound. Baste frequently with honey sauce (the end product of step 3).

3. Mix together in a small saucepan, ¼ cup honey, 2 tablespoons orange juice, 1 tablespoon grated orange peel, ¼ teaspoon allspice and ½ teaspoon dry mustard. Use to baste duckling while roasting.

4. After duckling has finished cooking remove to platter and keep hot by covering with aluminum foil. Pour off grease from roasting pan, leaving brown residue. To these drippings, blend in 1½ tablespoons cornstarch, 1 tablespoon grated orange peel and 1½ cups orange juice. Stir until it thickens. Remove to a sauce dish and serve with duckling.

5. Garnish platter of duckling with orange slices and parsely sprigs if you like.

Marinated Chicken Livers

Difficulty rating: VERY EASY

Equipment needed: Skillet & mixing bowl

Serves: 4

Estimated preparation time: 5-10 minutes

INGREDIENTS

1   pound chicken livers
1   jar soy sauce

⅓   cup all-purpose flour

4-6   strips bacon

BASIC STEPS

1. Marinate 1 pound of chicken livers overnight in soy sauce.

2. Drain the livers and dust with all-purpose flour.

3. In a skillet fry 4-6 strips of bacon until crisp. Drain on a paper towel and pour off excess grease.

4. Saute the chicken livers in remaining bacon grease for 5 minutes until nicely browned.

5. Crumple the bacon over livers and serve.

Notes:

Kitchen Tips ✓
The two best ways to put out a frying pan fire are to (1) slide (don't slam) a lid over the pan to deny it oxygen, and (2) pour baking soda directly on the flame.

Cornish Hen With Walnut Stuffing

Difficulty rating: EASY

Equipment needed: Roasting pan

Serves: 2

Estimated preparation time:
2 hours, approximately 1½ hours
of which is baking time

INGREDIENTS

2 Cornish hens (about 1 pound
each)
¼ cup vegetable oil
salt and pepper

1 cup milk
½ cup bread crumbs
4 tablespoons butter or
margarine
1 egg
salt and pepper
½ cup chopped walnuts

2 chicken bouillon cubes
2 cups water

3 tablespoons dry vermouth

BASIC STEPS

1. Thaw hens, rub with oil and salt
and pepper inside and out.

2. Pour 1 cup of milk into a mixing
bowl and combine with ½ cup
bread crumbs. Add in 4
tablespoons butter or margarine
and 1 well beaten egg. Salt and
pepper to taste and stir in ½ cup
chopped walnuts.

3. Dissolve 2 chicken bouillon
cubes in 2 cups water.

4. Stuff hens with walnut stuffing
and roast at 375⁰ for 1½ hours
basting frequently with bouillon.
Baste with dry vermouth last ½
hour.

Notes:

Honeyed Chicken

Difficulty rating: EASY

Equipment needed: Saucepan, mixing bowls & three-quart baking dish

Serves: 2-3

Estimated preparation time: 75-85 minutes

INGREDIENTS

1 cup wheat germ
2 teaspoons chopped parsely
¼ teaspoon basil
¼ teaspoon thyme
  salt and pepper

¾ cup honey
⅓ cup soy sauce
1 tablespoon vegetable oil
¼ teaspoon garlic powder
⅛ teaspoon ginger
1 tablespoon catsup

2 pounds of your favorite chicken parts

BASIC STEPS

1. Combine in a mixing bowl, 1 cup wheat germ, 2 teaspoons chopped parsely, ¼ teaspoon basil and ¼ teaspoon thyme. Salt and pepper to taste.

2. In a sauce pan, blend together over very low heat ¾ cup honey, ⅓ cup soy sauce, 1 tablespoon vegetable oil, ¼ teaspoon garlic powder ⅛ teaspoon ginger and 1 tablespoon catsup. Let simmer.

3. Dip the chicken parts in honeyed mix and then coat with wheat germ blend. Place in baking dish.

4. Pour the remaining honey mix over the chicken parts and bake at 375º for 45-60 minutes.

Notes:

Chicken Divan

Difficulty rating: EASY

Serves: 4-5

Equipment needed: Three-quart baking pan & 2 saucepans

Estimated preparation time: 65-75 minutes

INGREDIENTS

BASIC STEPS

1. Preheat oven at 400⁰.

3 chicken breasts

2. Place 3 chicken breasts in a baking pan, cover with aluminum foil, and bake in an oven at 400⁰ for 30-35 minutes until chicken is tender.

3. Remove from oven, let cool, and slice breasts into thin sections.

2 packages (10 ounces each) frozen broccoli

4. Prepare 2 packages (10 ounces each) frozen broccoli. Drain and set aside.

⅓ cup butter
⅓ cup all-purpose flour
2½ cups half & half cream
½ pound cheddar cheese

5. In a saucepan, blend together ⅓ cup butter, ⅓ cup all-purpose flour, 2½ cups half & half cream and ½ pound grated cheddar cheese.

6. Layer the bottom of a three-quart baking dish with broccoli. Cover this with a layer of chicken and pour sauce over the chicken and broccoli.

7. Bake for 20 minutes at 350⁰.

Notes:

Spiced Pork Chops

Difficulty rating: VERY EASY

Equipment needed: Large bowl & rack and broiler pan

Serves: 4

Estimated preparation time: 20-30 minutes

INGREDIENTS

⅓ cup soy sauce
½ teaspoon pepper
¼ teaspoon garlic powder
½ teaspoon marjoram
1 teaspoon sugar

4 pork chops

BASIC STEPS

1. In a bowl, combine ⅓ cup soy sauce, ½ teaspoon pepper, ¼ teaspoon garlic powder, ½ teaspoon marjoram and 1 teaspoon sugar.

2. Submerge 4 pork chops in the soy sauce mixture and marinate for 1 hour.

3. Arrange the chops on a rack in a broiler pan and broil each side for 10 minutes. Baste periodically with the marinade.

Notes:

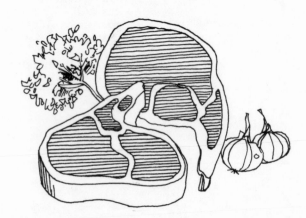

Baked Ham With Raisin Sauce

Difficulty rating: VERY EASY

Equipment needed: Roasting pan and saucepan

Serves: 6-8

Estimated preparation time:
3 hours, all but a few minutes of which is baking time

INGREDIENTS

1 ham (5-6 pounds)
  cloves

2 tablespoons butter
1 tablespoon brown sugar
3 tablespoons cornstarch
1½ cups apple cider
1 cup raisins
  allspice

BASIC STEPS

1. Place a 5-6 pound ham fat side up in a roasting pan. Insert 10-12 whole cloves over surface of ham.

2. Bake at 350° for 2 to 2½ hours. Baste with drippings every half hour.

3. While ham is cooking, make a raisin sauce as follows: Melt 2 tablespoons butter in saucepan. Stir in 1 tablespoon brown sugar, 3 tablespoons cornstarch, 1½ cups apple cider and 1 cup raisins. Continue to stir over medium heat until sauce thickens. Flavor to taste with allspice (start with just a dash).

4. When ham is done, remove cloves and cut desired number of slices.

5. Arrange slices on a platter and serve with raisin sauce.

Notes:

Short Ribs With Barbecue Sauce

Difficulty rating: VERY EASY

Equipment needed: Three-quart baking dish & bowl

Serves: 4-5

Estimated preparation time: 1½ to 2 hours

INGREDIENTS	BASIC STEPS
3-4 pounds short ribs	1. Place 3-4 pounds of beef short ribs in a shallow baking dish and brown ribs in a preheated oven at 500° for 30 minutes. Pour off fat.
1 bottle barbecue sauce 2 tablespoons brown sugar ¼ cup orange juice ½ cup pineapple chunks	2. In a separate bowl, blend together 1 bottle of your favorite barbecue sauce with 2 tablespoons brown sugar, ¼ cup orange juice and ½ cup pineapple chunks (optional).
	3. Pour the barbecue sauce over ribs and bake at 350° for 80-90 minutes until meat breaks off bone easily. Baste frequently
rice or noodles for 4-5 people	4. While meat is cooking, prepare rice or noodles for 4-5 people according to package directions or refer to page 192 for instructions on how to cook rice.

Notes:

130

Baked Ham Slices In Maple Syrup

Difficulty rating: VERY EASY

Equipment needed: Three-quart baking dish & mixing bowl

Serves: 1-2

Estimated preparation time: 60-70 minutes

INGREDIENTS

1 slice ham

1 cup maple syrup
¼ teaspoon allspice

BASIC STEPS

1. Place 1 slice of ham (about 1 inch thick) in a shallow baking pan.

2. In a small mixing bowl, blend together 1 cup maple syrup and ¼ teaspoon allspice.

3. Pour the syrup over the ham and bake at 325° for 50-60 minutes until ham is tender. Baste every 15-20 minutes.

Notes:

Pork Chops With Plum Sauce

Difficulty rating: VERY EASY

Equipment needed: Blender &
three-quart baking dish

Serves: 4

Estimated preparation time:
60-80 minutes

INGREDIENTS

1 can (28 ounces) plums
2 tablespoons honey
½ teaspoon allspice
½ cup red wine

4 pork chops

BASIC STEPS

1. In a blender, combine 1 can (28 ounces) plums, 2 tablespoons honey, ½ teaspoon allspice and ½ cup red wine. Puree until smooth.

2. Broil 4 pork chops until they are browned on both sides. Place the chops in a baking dish.

3. Pour plum sauce over chops and bake at 350º for 1 hour.

Notes:

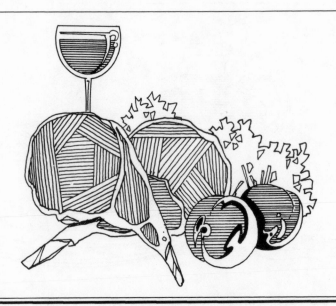

Pork Chops A L'Orange

Difficulty rating: VERY EASY

Equipment needed: Skillet & bowl

Serves: 4

Estimated preparation time:
50-60 minutes

INGREDIENTS

2 tablespoons butter or
  margarine
4 pork chops

1 orange
  cinnamon
  nutmeg

1 can (10½ ounces) condensed
  beef broth

¼ cup orange juice
1½ tablespoons cornstarch
1½ tablespoons brown sugar

BASIC STEPS

1. Heat 2 tablespoons butter or margarine in a skillet and brown 4 pork chops on both sides.

2. Slice an orange and place 1 piece on each chop. Sprinkle with cinnamon and nutmeg.

3. Add in 1 can (10½ ounces) condensed beef broth and let simmer for 30-35 minutes.

4. In a bowl, blend together ¼ cup orange juice , 1½ tablespoons cornstarch and 1½ tablespoons brown sugar.

5. Gently stir the orange juice mixture into the skillet with the chops until it thickens. Simmer another 10-15 minutes.

Notes:

Sweet and Sour Spareribs

Difficulty rating: EASY

Equipment needed: Roasting pan & skillet

Serves: 4

Estimated preparation time:
1½ hours, all but a few minutes of which is roasting time

INGREDIENTS

3-4 pounds of spareribs
   salt

1 clove of garlic
1 onion

2-3 tablespoons butter of margarine
¾ cup water
2 tablespoons soy sauce
¼ cup brown sugar
¼ cup vinegar
¼ cup catsup

BASIC STEPS

1. Preheat oven at 400°.

2. Arrange 3-4 pounds spareribs in a roasting pan, sprinkle with salt and roast 25-30 minutes.

3. While the ribs are cooking finely chop 1 clove of garlic and 1 onion.

4. Heat 2-3 tablespoons of butter or margarine in a skillet and saute onions and garlic for 5-7 minutes. Add in ¾ cup water, 2 tablespoons soy sauce, ¼ cup brown sugar, ¼ cup vinegar and ¼ cup catsup. Let simmer for 5 minutes.

5. After the ribs have cooked for 25-30 minutes, pour off excess fat and cover the ribs with the sweet and sour sauce produced in step 4.

6. Return to oven and roast for another 60-75 minutes.

Notes:

Spiced Hotdogs

Difficulty rating: VERY EASY

Equipment needed: Skillet & bowl

Serves: 4-5

Estimated preparation time:
25-30 minutes

INGREDIENTS

1½ cups water
2 tablespoons all-purpose flour
¾ cup catsup
2 tablespoons French-style
   mustard
1 tablespoon brown sugar
1 tablespoon vinegar

1 pound hotdogs

BASIC STEPS

1. In a bowl, combine 1½ cups
   water, 2 tablespoons all-purpose
   flour, ¾ cup catsup, 2 tablespoons
   French-style mustard, 1
   tablespoon brown sugar and 1
   tablespoon vinegar.

2. Slice 1 pound hotdogs in half
   lengthwise and place in a skillet.

3. Pour the liquid mixture over the
   hotdogs, cover and bring to a
   boil. Lower heat and simmer for
   about 20 minutes.

Notes:

Beef Stroganoff

Difficulty rating: EASY

Equipment needed: Skillet, large saucepan & bowl

Serves: 4

Estimated preparation time: 45-50 minutes

INGREDIENTS	BASIC STEPS
1½ pounds beef tenderloin or sirloin steak	1. Cut 1½ pounds of beef tenderloin or sirloin steak into 1½ x ½ inch strips.
½ cup onions 2 cups mushrooms	2. Chop ½ cup onions and slice 2 cups mushrooms.
2 tablespoons butter or margarine	3. Melt 2 tablespoons butter or margarine in a large skillet and saute onions for 5 minutes. Add the steak strips and cook until brown and tender.
	4. Stir in mushrooms and cook for 5 minutes.
1 can (10½ ounces) condensed beef bouillon ¼ cup red wine 3 tablespoons all-purpose flour 1 teaspoon dry mustard ¼ teaspoon garlic salt	5. In a bowl, combine 1 can (10½ ounces) condensed beef bouillon, ¼ cup red wine, 3 tablespoons all-purpose flour, 1 teaspoon dry mustard and ¼ teaspoon garlic salt. Pour over ingredients in skillet, cover and let simmer for 15-20 minutes.
1 package noodles	6. While meat mixture is simmering prepare noodles enough for 4 according to package directions.
1¼ cups sour cream	7. Just before serving, mix 1¼ cups sour cream into meat mixture and serve immediately over noodles.

Notes:

Pot Roast In Sour Cream

Difficulty rating: VERY EASY

Equipment needed: Roasting pan

Serves: 4-6

Estimated preparation time:
3 to 3½ hours, all but 5-10 minutes of which is baking time

INGREDIENTS

1 cup sour cream
¼ teaspoon onion salt
½ teaspoon marjoram

1 chuck roast (3-4 pounds)

BASIC STEPS

1. In a bowl, blend together 1 cup sour cream, ¼ teaspoon onion salt and ½ teaspoon marjoram.

2. Spread this mixture over a 3-4 pound chuck roast and wrap meat in aluminum foil so juices won't leak out.

3. Place on a roasting pan and bake at 300° for 3 to 3½ hours.

Notes:

137

Beef Burgundy

Difficulty rating: EASY

Serves: 4-6

Equipment needed: Skillet & bowl

Estimated preparation time: 2½ to 3 hours

INGREDIENTS

3 onions
½ pound mushrooms

2 tablespoons vegetable oil

2 pounds boneless chuck

1 cup Burgundy wine
2 tablespoons all-purpose flour
½ teaspoon thyme
salt and pepper

rice or noodles

BASIC STEPS

1. Chop 3 onions and slice ½ pound mushrooms.

2. Heat 2 tablespoons vegetable oil in a skillet and saute onions for 5 minutes. Add mushrooms and cook another 3-5 minutes. Drain, place vegetables in a separate bowl and set aside.

3. Cut 2 pounds of boneless chuck into bite size pieces and brown in the same skillet in which you cooked the onions and mushrooms.

4. Add in 1 cup Burgundy wine, 2 tablespoons all-purpose flour and ½ teaspoon thyme. Salt and pepper to taste. Simmer for 1½ to 2 hours until meat in tender.

5. Blend in the onions and mushrooms and simmer for another ½ hour.

6. While meat is cooking, prepare rice or noodles for 4-6 people according to directions on package. Or, refer to page 192 for instructions on how to cook rice.

7. Serve beef burgundy over rice or noodles.

Notes:

Ground Beef Stroganoff

Difficulty rating: EASY

Equipment needed: Skillet

Serves: 3-4

Estimated preparation time:
25-30 minutes

INGREDIENTS

1 onion
½ pound mushrooms

2 tablespoons vegetable oil

1 pound ground beef
  salt and pepper

1 cup sour cream

rice or noodles

BASIC STEPS

1. Chop 1 onion and slice ½ pound mushrooms.

2. Heat 2 tablespoons vegetable oil in a skillet and saute onions for 5 minutes. Add mushrooms and saute another 3-5 minutes.

3. Add in 1 pound ground beef and cook until meat is no longer red. Salt and pepper to taste.

4. Remove from heat and pour 1 cup sour cream over hamburger. Mix well, let simmer another 5-10 minutes.

5. While meat is cooking, prepare enough rice or noodles for 3-4 people according to directions on package. Or, refer to page 192 for instructions on how to cook rice.

6. Serve stroganoff over rice or noodles.

Notes:

Beef Stew

Difficulty rating: EASY

Equipment needed: Large kettle & skillet

Serves: 4-5

Estimated preparation time:
75-85 minutes, approximately 1 hour of which is cooking time.

INGREDIENTS

1 pound sirloin steak

2 onions
2 carrots
2 potatoes
2 ribs of celery

2 tablespoons vegetable oil

2½ cups beef bouillon broth
(use beef bouillion cubes)
2 tablespoons all-purpose flour

½ teaspoon thyme
½ teaspoon parsely
1 bay leaf
salt and pepper

BASIC STEPS

1. Cut 1 pound sirloin steak or chuck into bite size pieces.

2. Peel and cut into chunks 2 onions, 2 carrots and 2 potatoes. Chop 2 ribs of celery.

3. Heat 2 tablespoons vegetable oil in a skillet and saute onions for 5 minutes. Add meat chunks and cook until brown.

4. Transfer meat and onions to a large kettle.

5. Stir in 2½ cups beef bouillon broth and 2 tablespoons all-purpose flour.

6. Add the carrots, potatoes and celery.

7. Flavor with ½ teaspoon thyme, ½ teaspoon parsely, 1 bay leaf and salt and pepper to taste.

8. Let simmer on low heat for about 1 hour.

Notes:

Broiled Steak

Difficulty rating: VERY EASY

Serves: 1-2

Equipment needed: Broiling rack

Estimated preparation time: 10-15 minutes

INGREDIENTS

1-2 pounds steak 1 inch thick

salt and pepper
steak sauce

BASIC STEPS

1. Set oven on hot heat for broiling.

2. Place a 1-2 pound steak on a cutting board and slit outside edges every 3-4 inches to prevent curling.

3. Arrange the steak on a broiling rack and insert 3-4 inches from heat source.

4. Cook for 5, 7 or 9 minutes on each side for rare, medium or well done, respectively.

5. Salt and pepper to taste and serve hot with your favorite steak sauce.

Notes:

Meat Loaf

Difficulty rating: EASY

Equipment needed: Large mixing bowl & loaf pan (5 x 9 inches)

Serves: 5-6

Estimated preparation time:
2 hours, 1½ hours of which is baking time

INGREDIENTS

1½ pounds ground beef
1   tablespoon dry minced onions
2   tablespoons green pepper
1   cup bread crumbs
1   can (8 ounces) tomato sauce
1   egg
1   teaspoon salt
½   teaspoon pepper
½   teaspoon dry mustard
⅛   teaspoon garlic salt

BASIC STEPS

1. Preheat oven at 350°.

2. In a large bowl, mix together 1½ pounds ground beef with 1 tablespoon dry minced onions, 2 tablespoons finely chopped green peppers, 1 cup bread crumbs, 1 can (8 ounces) tomato sauce, 1 egg, 1 teaspoon salt, ½ teaspoon pepper, ½ teaspoon dry mustard and ⅛ teaspoon garlic salt.

3. When thoroughly mixed, shape into an oblong loaf and place in a 5 x 9 inch loaf pan.

4. Bake for 1½ hours.

Notes:

Kitchen Tips✓
For a "lighter" meat loaf, add ½ teaspoon of baking powder to the above recipe.

Sukiyaki

Difficulty rating: EASY

Equipment needed: Skillet

Serves: 4-6

Estimated preparation time: 45-60 minutes

INGREDIENTS	BASIC STEPS
1 pound beef sirloin	1. Cut 1 pound beef sirloin into 1½ x 1 inch strips.
2 onions 1 green pepper 2 ribs of celery 8 scallions	2. Slice 2 onions, cut 1 green pepper in rings, and cut 2 ribs of celery into thin strips 1½ inches in length. Also, cut 8 scallions into 1 inch sections, including green portion.
rice for 4-6 people	3. Begin to prepare enough rice for 4-6 people. Follow directions on package or refer to page 192 for instructions on how to cook rice.
¾ cup soy sauce ¼ cup sugar	4. In a bowl, combine ¾ cup soy sauce and ¼ cup sugar.
2 tablespoons butter or margarine	5. Heat 2 tablespoons butter or margarine in a skillet and brown steak strips lightly. Add the green peppers, onions and celery, and saute 3-4 minutes.
1 can (8 ounces) mushrooms 1 can (8 ounces) bamboo shoots	6. Add the soy sauce mixture and mix in 1 can (8 ounces) mushrooms, 1 can (8 ounces) bamboo shoots, and the scallions. Simmer another 5-7 minutes.
½ cup sake	7. Blend in ½ cup sake. Serve over rice.

Notes:

Chili With Wine

Difficulty rating: EASY

Equipment needed: Large soup kettle & skillet

Serves: 5-6

Estimated preparation time: 50-60 minutes

INGREDIENTS

1 onion
1 green pepper
1 cup mushrooms

2 tablespoons vegetable oil

1 pound ground beef
½ pound ground sausage

2 cans (15 ounces each) tomato sauce
1 can (16 ounces) tomatoes
½ cup water
¾ cup red wine

1 tablespoon chili powder
½ teaspoon cumin
½ teaspoon Tabasco sauce
½ teaspoon paprika
1 teaspoon garlic powder
1 teaspoon salt

2 cans (15 ounces each) kidney beans

crackers
red pepper

BASIC STEPS

1. Chop 1 onion, 1 green pepper and 1 cup mushrooms.

2. In a large skillet, heat 2 tablespoons vegetable oil and saute these vegetables over medium-hot heat for 5-10 minutes.

3. Stir in 1 pound ground beef and ½ pound ground sausage. Cook until beef is no longer red.

4. Transfer this mixture to large kettle. Add in 2 cans (15 ounces each) tomato sauce and 1 can tomatoes (16 ounces), ½ cup water and ¾ cup red wine.

5. Blend in 1 tablespoon chili powder, ½ teaspoon cumin, ½ teaspoon Tabasco sauce, ½ teaspoon paprika, 1 teaspoon garlic powder, and 1 teaspoon salt. Let simmer on low heat for 30 minutes.

6. Add 2 cans (15 ounces each) kidney beans and heat through for 5 minutes.

7. Serve in a bowl with crackers and red pepper on the side for those who like it hot. Also, a dollop of sour cream adds a nice touch.

Note: Freeze whatever is left for another meal or snack.

Stuffed Peppers

Difficulty rating: EASY

Equipment needed: Three-quart baking dish, skillet & bowl

Serves: 4

Estimated preparation time: 40-50 minutes

INGREDIENTS

4-6 green peppers

1 onion
½ cup sliced mushrooms

2 tablespoons butter or margarine

1½ pounds ground beef

8 ounces sour cream
4 ounces grated cheddar cheese
¼ teaspoon thyme
¼ teaspoon marjoram

BASIC STEPS

1. Preheat oven at 300°.

2. Wash and core 4-6 green peppers. Cover with water and boil for 10 minutes. Drain and set aside.

3. Chop 1 onion and slice ½ cup fresh mushrooms.

4. Heat 2 tablespoons butter or margarine and saute onions for 5 minutes. Add in 1½ pounds ground beef and the mushrooms and cook until meat is no longer red. Drain and set aside.

5. In a separate bowl, blend together 8 ounces sour cream, 4 ounces grated cheddar cheese, ¼ teaspoon thyme and ¼ teaspoon marjoram. Add to the skillet ingredients and mix thoroughly.

6. Stuff the peppers with the meat mixture and arrange in a shallow casserole dish. Bake for 30 minutes.

Notes:

Tacos

Difficulty rating: EASY

Equipment needed: Skillet, three-quart baking dish, mixing bowl & grater

Serves: 4-5

Estimated preparation time: 30-40 minutes

INGREDIENTS

1 head lettuce
2 green peppers
2 tomatoes
8-10 scallions

2 cups cheddar cheese
(about 8 ounces)

1 tablespoon vegetable oil
1 pound lean ground beef
1 package (1¼ ounce) taco seasoning mix*

10 taco shells

1 jar taco sauce

*Note: Taco shells, mix and sauce can be purchased at most supermarkets.

BASIC STEPS

1. Shred 1 head lettuce and chop 2 green peppers, 2 tomatoes and 8-10 scallions. Arrange separately on a platter.

2. Shred 2 cups cheddar cheese. Set aside.

3. In a skillet, heat 1 tablespoon vegetable oil and saute 1 pound lean ground beef over medium-hot heat until meat is no longer red. Blend in 1 package (1¼ ounces) taco seasoning mix.

4. Divide meat mixture evenly among 10 taco shells and top with a sprinkling of the cheddar cheese. Arrange in upright position in a shallow baking dish. Set under oven broiler 3-6 inches from heat source until cheese has melted.

5. Remove from oven and serve with vegetable toppings and taco sauce. Let each individual add his or her own toppings.

Notes:

Pizza

Difficulty rating: EASY

Equipment needed: 12-inch pizza pan & bowls

Serves: 4-5

Estimated preparation time:
Depends on options one employs; 35-45 minutes.

INGREDIENTS	BASIC STEPS
	1. Preheat oven at 450°.

Crust

2 packages (8 ounces each) refrigerated crescent dinner rolls	2-A. Spread 2 packages (8 ounces each) refrigerated crescent dinner rolls over a greased 12-inch pizza pan. Work the dough together and press toward the edge of the pan. Bake in a preheated oven at 375° for 8-10 minutes. The crust is now ready for sauce and toppings.
or	or
1 cup all-purpose flour 1 teaspoon baking powder ½ teaspoon salt ⅓ cup milk 1½ tablespoons vegetable oil	2-B. Combine in a bowl, 1 cup all-purpose flour, 1 teaspoon baking powder and ½ teaspoon salt. Add in ⅓ cup milk and 1½ tablespoons vegetable oil and mix until dough gathers into a ball. Knead dough for 2-3 minutes and then, on a floured surface, roll it into a 12-inch crust and place it on the pizza pan. Crust is now ready for sauce and toppings.

Sauce

1 jar pizza or spaghetti sauce	3-A. Open a jar of your favorite pizza or spaghetti sauce and spread evenly over crust.
or	or

Continued On Next Page

1 can (6 ounces) tomato sauce
⅛ teaspoon garlic salt
2 teaspoons oregano
1 teaspoon basil
2 teaspoons onion flakes

3-B. In a saucepan, mix together 1 can (6 ounces) tomato sauce, ⅛ teaspoon garlic salt, 2 teaspoons oregano, 1 teaspoon basil and 2 teaspoons dried onion flakes. Let simmer for 30 minutes. Spread evenly over crust.

Toppings

1 package (6 ounce) Mozzzarella cheese

4. Cover sauce with a layer of Mozzarella cheese (about 1 6-ounce package).

Choice of:
cooked and sliced Italian sausage , salami, pepperoni, tuna, sliced hot dogs, bologna, luncheon meats, anchovies, olives (green or black), sauteed onions, peppers or mushrooms

5. Top with any combination of the following: cooked and sliced Italian sausage, salami, pepperoni, tuna, sliced hot dogs, bologna, luncheon meats, anchovies, olives (green or black), sauteed onions, peppers or mushrooms.

grated Parmesan cheese

6. Sprinkle entire pizza with grated Parmesan cheese and bake for 20-25 minutes at 450°.

Notes:

Vegetables

Asparagus Hollandaise

Difficulty rating: VERY EASY

Equipment needed: Saucepan &
blender

Serves: 2-3

Estimated preparation time:
20-25 minutes

INGREDIENTS

hollandaise sauce

1 package (10 ounces) frozen
asparagus

BASIC STEPS

1. Open a jar of hollandaise sauce or
prepare your own according to
directions on page 198.

2. Cook 1 package (10 ounces)
frozen asparagus spears
according to directions.

3. Arrange asparagus spears on
serving plates and top with
hollandaise sauce.

Notes:

Asparagus-Cheese Casserole

Difficulty rating: EASY

Equipment needed: Casserole dish & saucepan

Serves: 4-5

Estimated preparation time: 45-50 minutes

INGREDIENTS

BASIC STEPS

1. Preheat oven at 350º.

2 packages (10 ounces each) frozen asparagus

2. Cook 2 packages (10 ounces each) frozen asparagus according to directions on package. Drain and transfer to a casserole dish.

¼ cup butter
¼ cup all-purpose flour
1½ cups milk

3. Melt ¼ cup butter in a saucepan and slowly blend in ¼ cup all-purpose flour. Add in 1½ cups milk and stir over low heat until thick.

½ cup white American cheese
½ cup cheddar cheese

4. Stir in ½ cup white American cheese and ½ cup cheddar cheese.

1 cup bread crumbs

5. Pour cheese mixture over asparagus, top with 1 cup bread crumbs and bake for 30 minutes.

6. Serve as a side dish.

Notes:

Baked Onions

Difficulty rating: VERY EASY

Equipment needed: Baking dish

Serves: Variable-one onion per person

Estimated preparation time:
60 minutes, all but a couple of minutes of which is baking time

INGREDIENTS

onions

butter
salt and pepper

BASIC STEPS

1. Preheat oven at 400°.

2. Place desired number of whole, unpeeled onions in a shallow baking dish.

3. Bake for 1 hour. Sprinkle with chips of butter, salt and pepper to taste and serve hot.

Notes:

Grilled Tomatoes

Difficulty rating: VERY EASY

Equipment needed: Shallow
baking dish

Serves: Variable-½ tomato per
person

Estimated preparation time:
15-20 minutes

INGREDIENTS

tomatoes

butter
salt
pepper
basil
grated Parmesan cheese

BASIC STEPS

1. Cut desired number of tomatoes
   in half.

2. Sprinkle the cut side of each
   tomato with pieces of butter, salt,
   pepper, basil and grated
   Parmesan cheese.

3. Arrange tomato halves in a
   shallow baking dish and broil
   until cheese melts (about 5-10
   minutes).

4. Serve hot.

Notes:

Artichoke-Spinach Casserole

Difficulty rating: EASY

Equipment needed: Bowl & casserole dish

Serves: 4

Estimated preparation time: 50-60 minutes

INGREDIENTS

2 packages (10 ounces each) frozen chopped spinach

1 jar artichoke hearts

⅓ cup milk
2 tablespoons butter or margarine
2 packages (3 ounces each) cream cheese

⅓ cup grated Parmesan cheese

BASIC STEPS

1. Preheat oven at 350⁰.

2. Thaw and drain 2 packages (10 ounces each) frozen chopped spinach.

3. Arrange 1 jar of artichoke hearts over the bottom of a casserole dish.

4. Distribute the spinach evenly over the artichoke hearts.

5. In a separate bowl, combine ⅓ cup milk, 2 tablespoons butter or margarine and 2 packages (3 ounces each) cream cheese.

6. Pour the milk mixture over spinach and artichokes and top with a heavy sprinkling of grated Parmesan cheese.

7. Bake for 35-40 minutes.

8. Serve as a side dish.

Notes:

Orange Glazed Beets

Difficulty rating: EASY

Equipment needed: Saucepan

Serves: 4

Estimated preparation time:
15-20 minutes

INGREDIENTS

1 tablespoon butter
1 tablespoon cornstarch

1 can (16 ounces) beets

2 tablespoons orange
  marmalade
1 tablespoon vinegar

BASIC STEPS

1. Melt 1 tablespoon butter in a
   saucepan and stir in 1
   tablespoon cornstarch.

2. Open 1 can (16 ounces) beets and
   pour ½ cup of liquid from beets
   into the saucepan. Stir slowly
   until thickened.

3. Blend in 2 tablespoons orange
   marmalade and 1 tablespoon
   vinegar.

4. Add the beets and simmer for
   8-10 minutes.

Notes:

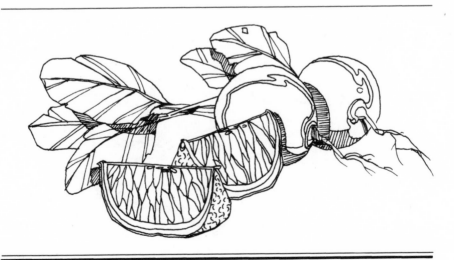

Green Beans In Sour Cream

Difficulty rating: VERY EASY

Equipment needed: 2 saucepans & mixing bowl

Serves: 4-6

Estimated preparation time: 15-20 minutes

INGREDIENTS

2 packages (10 ounces each) frozen green beans (French-style)

3 tablespoons butter
½ cup sour cream
2 tablespoons chives
1 teaspoon tarragon

BASIC STEPS

1. Prepare 2 packages (10 ounces each) frozen green beans (French-style) according to directions on package. Drain and transfer to a serving bowl.

2. In a small saucepan, melt 3 tablespoons butter, ½ cup sour cream, 2 tablespoons chives and 1 teaspoon tarragon. Simmer 3-5 minutes.

3. Pour sour cream sauce over beans and serve.

Notes:

Corn-On-The-Cob

Difficulty rating: VERY EASY

Equipment needed: Large kettle

Serves: variable 1-2 ears of corn per person

Estimated preparation time: 20 minutes

INGREDIENTS

1-2 ears of corn per person

½ cup melted butter
salt and pepper

*Note: For something a little different, blend together ½ cup melted butter and 1 tablespoon sherry.

BASIC STEPS

1. Remove the outer husks from the corn and wash thoroughly.

2. Place the corn into a kettle of unsalted boiling water and cook for 8-10 minutes.

3. Drain and serve with ½ cup melted butter and salt and pepper.*

Notes:

Kitchen Tips
Corn silk can be easily removed by rubbing the ear with a damp cloth.

Peppers Italian Style

Difficulty rating: VERY EASY

Equipment needed: Cake rack & mixing bowl

Serves: Variable

Estimated preparation time: 25-30

INGREDIENTS

4-6 green peppers

1 cup vegetable oil
¼ teaspoon garlic salt
1 tablespoon salt
1 teaspoon basil
1 teaspoon oregano
¼ teaspoon pepper

BASIC STEPS

1. Place 4-6 green peppers on a cake rack and roast in a preheated oven at 450° for 15 minutes. Remove and let cool.

2. In a bowl, combine 1 cup vegetable oil, ¼ teaspoon garlic salt, 1 tabespoon salt, 1 teaspoon basil, 1 teaspoon oregano and ¼ teaspoon pepper.

3. When peppers have cooled enough to handle, remove core and seeds and cut into thin strips.

4. Place the pepper strips in the marinade prepared in step 2 and marinate for 2-3 hours.

5. Serve as an accompaniment to Italian dishes. Also, include on antipasto platter.

Notes:

Cauliflower and Almonds

Difficulty rating: VERY EASY

Serves: 4-5

Equipment needed: 2 saucepans & casserole dish

Estimated preparation time: 15-20 minutes

INGREDIENTS

2 packages (10 ounces each) cauliflower

1 can (10½ ounces) condensed cream of mushroom soup

1 cup water
¼ cup slivered almonds

salt and pepper

butter
bread crumbs

BASIC STEPS

1. Cook 2 packages (10 ounces each) frozen cauliflower. Drain and put in a casserole.

2. Heat 1 can (10½ ounces) condensed cream of mushroom soup.

3. In a saucepan, boil 1 cup water and add ¼ cup slivered almonds. Cook for 2-3 minutes and drain.

4. Add the almonds to the soup and salt and pepper to taste. Pour the mixture over cauliflower.

5. Cover with some butter and a sprinkling of bread crumbs.

Notes:

Kitchen Tips ✓
When cooking cauliflower, add 1 tablespoon of milk to the water. This will help to retain a nice white color.

Baked Potatoes

Difficulty rating: VERY EASY

Equipment needed: None

Serve: Variable-1 per person

Estimated preparation time:
60 minutes, all but a couple of minutes of which is baking time.

INGREDIENTS

white potatoes

butter or margarine

butter
sour cream
bacon bits
chives

*Note: You might want to consider baking a few additional potatoes for later use as home fried or hash-brown potaotes.

BASIC STEPS

1. Scrub desired number of white potatoes with a brush.*

2. Rub skins with butter or margarine and prick with a fork.

3. Place in oven and bake at 400° for 50-60 minutes.

4. Serve with butter, sour cream, bacon bits and chives.

Notes:

Mashed Potatoes

Difficulty rating: EASY

Serves: 4

Equipment needed: Potato masher, saucepan & mixing bowl

Estimated preparation time: 30-40 minutes

INGREDIENTS

4 white potatoes

salt

¼-½ cup milk

2-3 tablespoons butter or margarine
salt and pepper

BASIC STEPS

1. Pare and quarter 4 white potatoes.

2. Drop the potatoes in a pan of boiling, salted water and cook for 20-25 minutes.

3. In a large bowl, mash potatoes, gradually adding milk, until smooth.

4. Blend in 2-3 tablespoons butter or margarine and salt and pepper to taste.

Notes:

Hash-Brown Potatoes

Difficulty rating: EASY

Equipment needed: Grater & skillet

Serves: 4

Estimated preparation time: 20-25 minutes

INGREDIENTS

3-4 cooked potatoes

2 tablespoons onions
2 tablespoons green peppers

2 tablespoons vegetable oil

salt and pepper

BASIC STEPS

1. Shred 3-4 cooked potatoes. Pare skin off or leave on as you prefer.

2. Finely chop 2 tablespoons onions and 2 tablespoons green peppers.

3. Heat 2 tablespoons vegetable oil in a skillet and saute onions and peppers 4-5 minutes.

4. Add in potatoes and fry until nicely browned (about 15-20 minutes). Salt and pepper to taste.

Notes:

Home Fried Potatoes

Difficulty rating: EASY

Equipment needed: Skillet

Serves: 4

Estimated preparation time:
20-25 minutes

INGREDIENTS	BASIC STEPS
4 cooked potatoes	1. Slice 4 cooked potatoes. Pare skin off or leave it on as you prefer.
2 scallions 2 tablespoons green pepper	2. Finely chop 2 scallions (include green part) and 2 tablespoons green pepper.
2 tablespoons vegetable oil	3. Heat 2 tablespoons vegetable oil in a skillet and saute onions and peppers 4-5 minutes.
salt and pepper	4. Add in potatoes and fry until nicely browned (about 20 minutes). Salt and pepper to taste.

Notes:

Kitchen Tips ✓
"Spattering" can be kept to a minimum by sprinkling a little salt into the skillet.

German Potato Salad

Difficulty rating: EASY

Equipment needed: Large kettle & skillet

Serves: 4-5

Estimated preparation time: 50-60 minutes.

INGREDIENTS

6 potatoes
1 teaspoon salt

6 slices bacon

4 scallions

2 tablespoons flour
3 tablespoons honey
1 teaspoon celery seed
   salt and pepper
1 cup water
½ cup vinegar

1 jar pimientos.

BASIC STEPS

1. In a pan of boiling salted (1 teaspoon) water, drop 6 potatoes and cook until done (about 30-40 minutes). Drain and slice with or without skins as preferred.

2. Cook 6 slices bacon in a large skillet until crisp. Place on paper towel to drain. Crumble when cool.

3. Pour off most of the bacon grease. Chop and saute 4 scallions in reserve grease for about 3 minutes.

4. Reduce heat to low and blend in 2 tablespoons flour, 3 tablespoons honey, 1 teaspoon celery seed and salt and pepper to taste. Add 1 cup water and ½ cup vinegar.

5. Add crumbled bacon and potatoes to mixture. Continue to cook another 10-15 minutes.

6. Garnish with chopped pimientos.

Notes:

Breads, Pastries and Desserts

Drop Biscuits

Difficulty rating: VERY EASY

Equipment needed: Baking sheet & bowl

Serves: 12-14 biscuits

Estimated preparation time: 20-25 minutes

INGREDIENTS

2 cups all-purpose flour
1 tablespoon baking powder
½ teaspoon salt

⅓ cup shortening
1 cup milk

BASIC STEPS

1. Preheat oven to 450º.

2. In a bowl, combine 2 cups all-purpose flour with 1 tablespoon baking powder and ½ teaspoon salt.

3. Work in ⅓ cup shortening and add 1 cup milk. Mix well.

4. Drop batter by the teaspoon onto an ungreased baking sheet.

5. Bake about 12-15 minutes.

Notes:

Plain Muffins

Difficulty rating: EASY

Equipment needed: Twelve-unit muffin pan & 2 mixing bowls

Serves: Makes 12 muffins

Estimated preparation time: 25-30 minutes

INGREDIENTS

2 cups all-purpose flour
1 teaspoon salt
1 tablespoon baking powder
¼ cup sugar

1 cup milk
¼ cup vegetable oil
1 egg

BASIC STEPS

1. Preheat oven to 425°.

2. Combine in a bowl, 2 cups all-purpose flour, 1 teaspoon salt, 1 tablespoon baking powder and ¼ cup sugar.

3. In another bowl, mix 1 cup milk, ¼ cup vegetable oil and 1 well beaten egg.

4. Add to dry mixture, stir only until uniformly moist.

5. Grease a twelve-unit muffin pan and fill each cup about ⅔ full with batter.

6. Bake 15-20 minutes.

Notes:

Three-Grain Muffins

Difficulty rating: EASY

Equipment needed: 2 bowls & twelve-unit muffin pan

Serves: Yields 12 muffins

Estimated preparation time: 30-40 minutes

INGREDIENTS

1 cup whole wheat flour
1 cup yellow corn meal
½ cup dark rye flour
½ teaspoon salt
2 teaspoons baking powder

2 eggs
1½ cups milk
¼ cup honey
¼ cup vegetable oil

BASIC STEPS

1. Preheat oven at 400º.

2. In a bowl, mix together 1 cup whole wheat flour, 1 cup yellow corn meal, ½ cup dark rye flour, ½teaspoon salt and 2 teaspoons baking powder.

3. In a separate bowl, beat 2 eggs and mix in 1½ cups milk, ¼ cup honey and ¼ cup vegetable oil.

4. Pour liquid mixture into the dry one and mix thoroughly.

5. Grease a 12-unit muffin pan and fill each unit about ⅔ full with the batter.

6. Bake for 20 minutes.

Notes:

White Bread

Difficulty rating: EASY

Equipment needed: 2 9 x 5 inch loaf pans & mixing bowl

Serves: Makes 2 loaves

Estimated preparation time:
3 to 3½ hours, most of which is the time it takes for the dough to rise

INGREDIENTS

½ cup warm water
2 packages active dry yeast

2 cups milk
½ cup melted butter or margarine
½ cup honey
2 eggs
1 teaspoon salt

7-8 cups all-purpose flour

BASIC STEPS

1. Pour ½ cup warm water into a large mixing bowl and sprinkle with 2 packages of active dry yeast. Let sit for about 5 minutes.

2. To the water and yeast mixture, add 2 cups milk, ½ cup melted butter or margarine, ½ cup honey, 2 eggs and 1 teaspoon salt. Mix well.

3. Gradually blend in 7 to 8 cups all-purpose flour until dough clumps together. Knead the dough on a floured board for 5-10 minutes.

4. Place dough in a lightly greased bowl, cover with a towel and let rise in a warm place* for 1½ hours, until double its original bulk.

5. Punch dough down and divide into equal halves. Shape and fit into 2 loaf pans (5 x 9 inches) and let dough rise again for 1 hour.

6. Bake in a preheated oven at 400° for 15 minutes. Lower heat to 350° and bake another 20-30 minutes. Brush with butter.

*Note: Any place near a heat source is good. Also, you can place the bowl on top of a television set or set it in an oven with a pan of hot water.

Whole Wheat Bread

Difficulty rating: EASY

Equipment needed: 2 9 x 5 inch loaf pans & bowl

Serves: Makes 2 loaves

Estimated preparation time:
3 to 3½ hours, most of which is the time it takes for the dough to rise

INGREDIENTS

2½ cups warm water
 2 packages active dry yeast

½ cup melted butter or margarine
½ cup honey
 2 eggs
 1 teaspoon salt

6-7 cups whole wheat flour

BASIC STEPS

1. Pour 2½ cups warm water into a large mixing bowl and sprinkle with 2 packages of active dry yeast. Let sit for about 5 minutes.

2. To the water and yeast mixture, add ½ cup melted butter or margarine, ½ cup honey, 2 lightly beaten eggs and 1 teaspoon salt. Mix well.

3. Gradually blend in 6 to 7 cups whole wheat flour until dough clumps together. Knead dough on a floured board for 5-10 minutes.

4. Place dough in a lightly greased bowl, cover with towel and let rise in a warm place* for 1½ hours, until double its original bulk.

5. Punch dough down and divide into equal halves. Shape and fit into 2 loaf pans and let dough rise again for 1 hour.

6. Bake in a preheated oven at 375° about 45 minutes.

*Note: Any place near a heat source is good. Also, you can place the bowl on top of a television set or set it in an oven with a pan of hot water.

Rye Bread

Difficulty rating: EASY

Serves: Makes 2 loaves

Equipment needed: 2 9 x 5 inch loaf pans & large mixing bowl

Estimated preparation time:
3 to 3½ hours, most of which is the time it takes for the dough to rise

INGREDIENTS

2 cups water
2 packages active dry yeast

2 tablespoons melted butter or margarine
½ cup brown sugar
1 teaspoon salt
2 tablespoons caraway seeds

3 cups all-purpose flour
2-3 cups rye flour

*Note: Any place near a heat source is good. Also, you can place the bowl on top of a television set or set it in an oven with a pan of hot water.

BASIC STEPS

1. Pour 2 cups warm water into a large mixing bowl and sprinkle with 2 packages of active dry yeast. Let sit for 5 minutes.

2. To the water and yeast mixture, add 2 tablespoons melted butter or margarine, ½ cup brown sugar, 1 teaspoon salt and 2 tablespoons caraway seeds.

3. In a separate bowl, blend together 3 cups all-purpose flour and 2-3 cups rye flour.

4. Gradually add the combined flours to the liquid mixture until dough clumps together. Knead dough on a floured board for 5-10 minutes.

5. Place dough in a lightly greased bowl, cover with a towel and let rise in a warm place* for 1½ hours until double its original bulk.

6. Punch dough down and divide into equal halves. Shape and fit into 2 loaf pans and let dough rise again for 1 hour.

7. Bake in preheated oven at 350° for 40-45 minutes.

Pumpkin Bread

Difficulty rating: EASY

Equipment needed: 2 9x5 inch loaf pans & large mixing bowl

Serves: Makes 2 loaves

Estimated preparation time: 70-80 minutes

INGREDIENTS

3 cups all-purpose flour
3 cups sugar
1 can (16 ounces) pumpkin pie filling
1 cup vegetable oil
1 cup seedless raisins
1 teaspoon baking soda
1 teaspoon nutmeg
1 teaspoon cinnamon
1 teaspoon ground cloves
1 teaspoon salt

4 eggs

BASIC STEPS

1. Preheat oven at 350º.

2. In a large mixing bowl, combine 3 cups all-purpose flour, 3 cups sugar, 1 can (16 ounces) pumpkin pie filling, 1 cup vegetable oil, 1 cup seedless raisins, 1 teaspoon baking soda, 1 teaspoon nutmeg, 1 teaspoon cinnamon, 1 teaspoon ground cloves and 1 teaspoon salt.

3. In a separate bowl, beat 4 eggs and add to pumpkin mixture. Stir well.

4. Pour batter into 2 greased and floured pans and bake for 1 hour.

Notes:

Kitchen Tips
In kneading bread dough oil your hands a little and it will prevent them from sticking to the dough.

Zucchini Bread

Difficutly rating: EASY

Equipment needed: 2 9 x 5 inch loaf pans, 2 large mixing bowls & grater

Serves: Makes 2 loaves

Estimated preparation time: 75-80 minutes

INGREDIENTS

2 cups zucchini
1 cup walnuts

3½ cups all-purpose flour
1 teaspoon salt
1 teaspoon baking soda
½ teaspoon baking powder
1 teaspoon nutmeg
1 tablespoon cinnamon

4 eggs
1 cup vegetable oil
1½ cups honey
2 teaspoons vanilla

BASIC STEPS

1. Preheat oven at 350⁰.

2. Peel and shred 2 cups zucchini and chop 1 cup walnuts.

3. In a large mixing bowl, combine 3½ cups all-purpose flour, 1 teaspoon baking soda, ½ teaspoon baking powder, 1 teaspoon nutmeg and 1 tablespoon cinnamon.

4. In a separate bowl, beat 4 eggs and mix together with 1 cup vegetable oil, 1½ cups honey and 2 teaspoons vanilla. Add in the zucchini.

5. Add the dry ingredients and walnuts and mix well.

6. Pour batter into 2 greased loaf pans and bake for 1 hour.

Notes:

173

Drop Cookies

Difficulty rating: VERY EASY

Equipment needed: Baking sheet & bowl

Serves: Yields 20-24 cookies

Estimated preparation time: 15-20 minutes

INGREDIENTS

1 cup softened butter
1 cup sugar

2 eggs
1 teaspoon vanilla
2 tablespoons milk

2 cups all-purpose flour
1 teaspoon baking powder

BASIC STEPS

1. Preheat oven at 375°.

2. In a large bowl, blend together 1 cup softened butter and 1 cup sugar.

3. Beat 2 eggs and add to butter and sugar mixture. Also, work in 1 teaspoon vanilla and 2 tablespoons milk.

4. In a separate bowl, mix together 2 cups all-purpose flour and 1 teaspoon baking powder. Combine with other ingredients. Mix thoroughly.

5. Drop batter one teaspoon at a time and 1 inch apart on a lightly greased baking sheet and sprinkle with sugar.

6. Bake for 8-10 minutes.

Notes:

Oatmeal Cookies

Difficulty rating: EASY

Equipment needed: Baking sheet & bowl

Serves: Yields about 36 cookies

Estimated preparation time: 25-30 minutes

INGREDIENTS

½	cup whole wheat flour
¾	cup all purpose flour
2	cups uncooked rolled oats
1	teaspoon cinnamon
½	teaspoon allspice
½	teaspoon ginger
½	teaspoon baking powder
1	teaspoon baking soda
½	teaspoon salt
2	eggs
¼	cup unsulphured molasses
½	cup honey
½	cup vegetable oil
1	teaspoon vanilla
1	cup raisins

BASIC STEPS

1. Preheat oven at 400°.

2. In a bowl, combine ½ cup whole wheat flour, ¾ cup all purpose flour, 2 cups uncooked rolled oats, 1 teasponn cinnamon, ½ teaspoon allspice, ½ teaspoon ginger, ½ teaspoon baking powder, 1 teaspoon baking soda and ½ teaspoon salt.

3. In a separate bowl, beat 2 eggs and mix together with ¼ cup unsulphured molasses, ½ cup honey, ½ cup vegetable oil and 1 teaspoon vanilla.

4. Pour the liquid mixture into the dry ingredients and mix thoroughly. Add in 1 cup raisins and let stand 10-15 minutes.

5. Drop batter, a spoonful at a time onto a lightly greased baking sheet and bake for 8-10 minutes, until nicely brown.

Notes:

Brownies

Difficulty rating: EASY

Equipment needed: Mixing bowl, saucepan & 8 x 8 x 2 inch baking dish

Serves: Makes about 16 brownies

Estimated preparation time: 60-70 minutes

INGREDIENTS

¾ cup butter
¼ pound unsweetened chocolate

6 eggs
1½ cups sugar

¾ cup all-purpose flour
2 teaspoons vanilla
1 cup chopped walnuts

2 tablespoons butter
¼ cup milk
6 ounces semi-sweet chocolate chips

BASIC STEPS

1. Preheat oven at 350°.

2. In a saucepan, melt ¾ cup butter together with ¼ pound unsweetened chocolate.

3. Beat 6 eggs and combine with 1½ cups sugar in a large mixing bowl. Blend in the butter and chocolate mixture and stir.

4. Then, one at a time, add in ¾ cup all-purpose flour, 2 teaspoons vanilla, and 1 cup chopped walnuts. Stir just enough to moisten flour.

5. Pour batter into baking dish and bake for 30 minutes.

6. Cool and serve plain or cover with the icing produced in step 7.

7. Melt together in a saucepan over medium-low heat, 2 tablespoons butter, ¼ cup milk and 6 ounces semi-sweet chocolate chips. When ingredients have been uniformly combined spread evenly over brownies.

Notes:

Blueberry Cake

Difficulty rating: EASY

Equipment needed: 9 x 9 inch baking dish & 2 bowls

Serves: 8-10

Estimated preparation time: 60 minutes

INGREDIENTS

¾ cup honey
½ cup butter
2 eggs

1⅔ cups whole wheat flour
¼ teaspoon salt
1½ teaspoons baking powder
½ cup milk

1 cup fresh blueberries

powdered sugar

BASIC STEPS

1. Preheat oven at 375º.

2. In a bowl, beat together ¾ cup honey, ½ cup melted butter and 2 eggs.

3. In a separate bowl, blend together 1⅔ cups whole wheat flour, ¼ teaspoon salt, 1½ teaspoons baking powder and ½ cup milk. Mix thoroughly.

4. Combine the two mixtures and work in 1 cup fresh blueberries.

5. Pour into baking dish and bake for 40-45 minutes.

6. Top with a sprinkling of powdered sugar and serve.

Notes:

Carrot Cake

Difficulty rating: EASY

Serves: Variable-about 10-12

Equipment needed: 2 large mixing bowls, twelve-cup tube pan & grater

Estimated preparation time: 70-80 minutes

INGREDIENTS

3 cups carrots
1 cup English walnuts

2 cups sugar
2 cups whole wheat flour
2 teaspoons baking powder
1 teaspoon baking soda
1 teaspoon salt
2 teaspoons cinnamon

4 eggs

1½ cups vegetable oil

powdered sugar

BASIC STEPS

1. Preheat oven at 350º.

2. Grate 3 cups carrots and chop 1 cup English walnuts.

3. In a large mixing bowl, combine 2 cups sugar, 2 cups whole wheat flour, 2 teaspoons baking powder, 1 teaspoon baking soda, 1 teaspoon salt and 2 teaspoons cinnamon.

4. In a separate bowl, beat 4 eggs and add to dry mixture.

5. Blend in 1½ cups vegetable oil and add the carrots and nuts. Mix well.

6. Transfer to greased tube pan and bake for 50 minutes.

7. Serve plain or with powdered sugar.

Notes:

Kitchen Tips
When you have trouble getting a cake out of the pan, try holding the pan over a low flame for a few seconds. The cake should drop right out.

Bread Pudding

Difficulty rating: VERY EASY

Serves: 4

Equipment needed: Mixing bowl & casserole dish

Estimated preparation time: 50-60 minutes

INGREDIENTS

BASIC STEPS

1. Preheat oven at 400°.

5-6 cups stale bread

2. Break 5-6 cups of stale bread into small pieces and place in a casserole.

  3 eggs
¾ cup milk
¾ cup sugar
  2 teaspoons vanilla
½ teaspoon cinnamon
¼ teaspoon nutmeg

3. In a separate bowl, combine 3 well beaten eggs, ¾ cup milk, ¾ cup sugar, 2 teaspoons vanilla, ½ teaspoon cinnamon and ¼ teaspoon nutmeg.

4. Pour the liquid mixture over the bread and let stand for 10 minutes.

½ cup raisins

5. Blend in ½ cup raisins and set casserole in a pan of water and bake for 35-40 minutes.

6. Serve plain or with milk or cream.

Notes:

Chocolate-Brandy Dessert

Difficulty rating: VERY EASY

Equipment needed: Blender

Serves: 3-4

Estimated preparation time:
5-10 minutes

INGREDIENTS

1   pint chocolate ice cream
⅓ cup brandy

¼ cup chocolate shavings

BASIC STEPS

1. Spoon 1 pint chocolate ice cream into a blender and add in ⅓ cup brandy. Mix thoroughly.

2. Serve in a goblet or wide neck glass. Garnish with a sprinkling of chocolate shavings.

Notes:

Banana Flambé

Difficulty rating: MODERATELY
EASY

Equipment needed: 2 saucepans

Serves: 4

Estimated preparation time:
20-25 minutes

INGREDIENTS

4 bananas

¼ cup butter
½ cup honey

⅓ cup banana liqueur
cinnamon
nutmeg

½ cup brandy
1 quart vanilla ice cream

BASIC STEPS

1. Peel 4 bananas and cut into bite
size pieces.

2. Melt ¼ cup butter in a skillet and
add in ½ cup honey. Bring to a
boil.

3. Reduce heat, add bananas and
simmer for 5-7 minutes. Add in
⅓ cup banana liqueur and flavor
with cinnamon and nutmeg to
taste.

4. In a separate saucepan, warm ½
cup brandy and pour over the
banana mixture. Ignite with a
match and when flame burns
out, spoon over 4 bowls of vanilla
ice cream.

Notes:

Banana Cream Pie

Difficulty rating: EASY

Serves: 4-6

Equipment needed: 1 9 inch pie pan & mixing bowl

Estimated preparation time: 30-40 minutes

INGREDIENTS	BASIC STEPS
1 graham cracker pie shell (9 inches)	1. Prepare 1 9-inch graham cracker pie crust. You can purchase a frozen shell or refer to page 195 for instructions on how to make your own.
1 package (3¼ ounces) instant banana pudding 1 cup milk 1 pint ice cream	2. In a large mixing bowl, combine 1 package (3¼ ounces) instant banana pudding mix with 1 cup milk and blend in 1 pint vanilla ice cream.
1 banana	3. Slice 1 banana and arrange the slices over the bottom of pie shell.
1 banana	4. Pour the pudding-ice cream mixture over the bananas and top with a few slices of bananas.
whipped cream	5. Chill until filling firms up and serve as is or with whipped cream.

Notes:

Mock Cheesecake

Difficulty rating: EASY

Equipment needed: Blender & 1 9-inch pie pan

Serves: 6

Estimated preparation time: 30-40 minutes

INGREDIENTS

½ teaspoon grated lemon rind

12 ounces (1½ 8-ounce packages) cream cheese
¼ cup sour cream
¼ cup honey
2 eggs
1 tablespoon vanilla
1 teaspoon lemon juice

1 9-inch graham cracker pie shell

1 can cherry or blueberry pie filling

BASIC STEPS

1. Preheat oven at 375⁰.

2. Grate ½ teaspoon lemon rind.

3. In a blender, combine 12 ounces (1½ 8-ounce packages) cream cheese, ¼ cup sour cream, ¼ cup honey, 2 eggs, 1 tablespoon vanilla, 1 teaspoon lemon juice and the grated lemon rind.

4. Make ready a 9-inch graham cracker pie shell. You can purchase a ready made shell or refer to page 195 for instructions on how to make your own.

5. Pour the blended ingredients into the pie shell and bake for 20 minutes.

6. Chill and serve topped with a tablespoon of cherry or blueberry pie filling.

Notes:

Ice Cream Grasshopper Dessert

Difficulty rating: VERY EASY

Equipment needed: Blender

Serves: 3-4

Estimated preparation time:
5-10 minutes

INGREDIENTS

1 quart vanilla ice cream
1½ ounces creme de cocao
1½ ounces green creme de
    menthe

Note: After trying this a time or two,
adjust to own taste.

BASIC STEPS

1. Combine in a blender, 5 scoops
   vanilla ice cream, 1½ ounces
   creme de cacao and 1½ ounces
   green creme de menthe.

2. Serve in wide neck wine glasses
   or goblets.

Notes:

Peaches In Sour Cream

Difficulty rating: EASY

Equipment needed: 4 ovenproof bowls, mixing bowl & shallow broiler pan

Serves: 4

Estimated preparation time: 15-20 minutes

INGREDIENTS

5-6 fresh peaches

¼ cup brown sugar
1 teaspoon cinnamon

1 cup sour cream
4 tablespoons sugar

BASIC STEPS

1. Peel and slice 5-6 fresh peaches.

2. Divide sliced peaches evenly among 4 ovenproof bowls.

3. In a separate bowl, mix together ¼ cup brown sugar and 1 teaspoon cinnamon. Sprinkle over peaches.

4. Cover each bowl of peaches with 2-3 tablespoons sour cream and top with 1 tablespoon of sugar.

5. Place the 4 bowls on a shallow broiling pan and place under a broiler until the sugar melts (about 2-4 minutes).

6. Serve immediately.

Notes:

Banana-Coffee Dessert

Difficulty rating: VERY EASY

Equipment needed: Blender

Serves: 2

Estimated preparation time:
5-10 minutes

INGREDIENTS

2 teaspoons instant coffee

1 pint vanilla ice cream
1 banana

cinnamon

BASIC STEPS

1. Prepare 1 cup of instant coffee using cold water and 2 teaspoons coffee.

2. In a blender, combine coffee, 4 scoops vanilla ice cream and 1 banana.

3. Serve in wide neck wine glasses. Top with a dash of cinnamon.

Notes:

Cinnamon Pears

Difficulty rating: VERY EASY

Equipment needed: Small saucepan

Serves: 2

Estimated preparation time: 20 minutes

INGREDIENTS

2 pears

1½ cups apple cider
2 tablespoons honey
½ teaspoon cinnamon

2-3 tablespoons whipped cream
slivered almonds

BASIC STEPS

1. Peel two pears, cut them in half lengthwise and remove core.

2. In a saucepan, combine 1½ cups apple cider, 2 tablespoons honey and ½ teaspoon cinnamon. Add pears. Simmer 10-15 minutes and set aside to cool.

3. When room temperature, remove from pan and arrange 2 pear halves on a dish with cored side up. Drop a tablespoon of whipped cream on top and sprinkle with slivered almonds.

Notes:

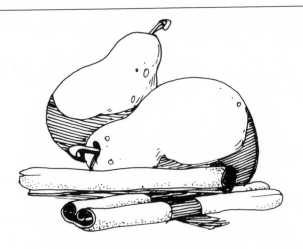

Cheese Loaf Dessert

Difficulty rating: EASY

Equipment needed: 5 x 9 inch loaf pan & 2 mixing bowls

Serves: 6-8

Estimated preparation time:
60-70 minutes

INGREDIENTS

½ cup softened butter
¼ cup honey
3 eggs
¾ cup milk
1¼ cups whole wheat flour
1 teaspoon baking powder
½ teaspoon salt

1 pound Ricotta cheese
1 egg
¼ teaspoon sugar

1 cup sour cream
cinnamon

BASIC STEPS

1. Preheat oven at 350º.

2. In a bowl, blend together ½ cup softened butter, ¼ cup honey, 3 eggs, ¾ cup milk, 1¼ cups whole wheat flour, 1 teaspoon baking powder and ½ teaspoon salt.

3. Combine in a separate bowl, 1 pound Ricotta cheese, 1 well beaten egg and ¼ teaspoon sugar.

4. Grease a 5 x 9 inch loaf pan and pour half the batter prepared in step 1 into the pan.

5. Layer in the Ricotta cheese mixture and cover with the other half of the batter.

6. Bake for 45-50 minutes.

7. Serve hot with 1-2 teaspoons sour cream and a sprinkling of cinnamon.

Notes:

Kitchen Tips✓
You can substitute cottage cheese for Ricotta in cooking. This will save you a little money and the fat content is lower.

Basics

Basic White Sauce

Difficulty rating: EASY

Equipment needed: Saucepan

Serves: Variable-makes about 1½ cups

Estimated preparation time: 10-15 minutes

INGREDIENTS	BASIC STEPS
2 tablespoons butter	1. Melt 2 tablespoons butter in a saucepan over low heat.
¼ cup all-purpose flour	2. Stir in ¼ cup all-purpose flour for 1 minute.
1 cup milk	3. Remove from heat and slowly blend in 1 cup milk.
salt and pepper	4. Return to heat and allow mixture to come to a boil. Continue to stir for 1-2 minutes until thick and smooth. Salt and pepper to taste.

Notes:

Garlic Bread

Difficulty rating: VERY EASY

Equipment needed: Bowl & pastry brush

Serves: 5-6

Estimated preparation time: 15-20 minutes

INGREDIENTS

1 clove garlic

½ cup butter

1 loaf French bread

¼ cup grated parmesan cheese

BASIC STEPS

1. Preheat oven at 400º.

2. Finely chop 1 clove of garlic.

3. In a saucepan, melt ½ cup butter and blend in the minced garlic.

4. Slice 1 loaf of French bread into ¾-1 inch slices, leaving the bottom crust intact.

5. Brush both sides of each slice of bread with garlic butter and sprinkle with grated parmesan cheese.

7. Bake for 8-10 minutes and serve warm.

Notes:

Cooking Rice

Difficulty rating: EASY

Equipment needed: Covered pan or kettle

Serves: Variable

Estimated preparation time: 40-50 minutes

INGREDIENTS	BASIC STEPS
	Regular White Rice
2 cups water 1 cup regular white rice ½ teaspoon salt	1. In a 2-quart pan, heat 2 cups water, 1 cup regular white rice, and ½ teaspoon salt to boiling. Reduce heat to low, cover and let simmer for about 14 minutes, until rice has absorbed liquid. **Do not stir while the rice is cooking.** Yields about 3 cups of cooked rice.
	Brown Rice
2 cups water 1 cup brown rice ½ teaspoon salt	1. Follow the same directions for cooking regular white rice (above) but extend the cooking time to 40-45 minutes. Yields about 3-3½ cups of cooked rice.
	Wild Rice
2 cups water 1 cup wild rice ½ teaspoon salt	1. Rinse rice carefully under cold water. Follow the same directions for cooking brown rice (above). Yields about 3-3½ cups cooked rice.

Notes:

Tomato Sauce (Meatless)

Difficulty rating: EASY

Equipment needed: Large skillet & sieve

Serves: Variable-makes about 1 pint

Estimated preparation time: 50-60 minutes

INGREDIENTS

1 onion
½ green pepper
1 cup mushrooms
1 clove garlic

2 tablespoons olive oil

1 can (2pounds)tomatoes
¼ cup tomato paste
1 teaspoon basil
1 teaspoon oregano
½ teaspoon sugar
2 tablespoons parsely

salt and pepper

BASIC STEPS

1. Chop 1 onion and ½ green pepper. Slice 1 cup mushrooms and finely chop 1 clove garlic.

2. Heat 2 tablespoons olive oil in a large skillet and saute onions, peppers, and garlic 5 minutes. Add mushrooms and cook another 3 minutes.

3. Add 1 can (2 pounds) tomatoes, ¼ cup tomato paste, 1 teaspoon basil, 1 teaspoon oregano, ½ teaspoon sugar and 2 tablespoons parsley.

4. Let simmer for 30-40 minutes stirring often. Salt and pepper to taste.

5. The sauce can be usesd as is, or, if you prefer, strain it through a sieve squeezing down on residue with a wooden spoon.

6. Serve with grated cheese over any kind of pasta.

Note: This is a basic recipe. Don't be afraid to experiment on your own gradually adding and subtracting ingredients according to your taste preferences.

Notes:

Tomato Sauce (With Meat)

Difficulty rating: EASY

Equipment needed: Large skillet

Serves: Variable-makes about 1 quart

Estimated preparation time: 60-70 minutes

INGREDIENTS	BASIC STEPS
1 onion ½ green pepper 1 cup mushrooms 2 finely chopped cloves garlic	1. Chop 1 onion and ½ green pepper. Slice 1 cup mushrooms and finely chop 2 cloves garlic.
2 tablespoons olive oil	2. Heat 2 tablespoons olive oil in a large skillet and saute onions, peppers and garlic for 5 minutes. Add mushrooms and cook another 3 minutes.
1 pound ground beef ½ pound ground sausage	3. Add 1 pound ground beef and ½ pound ground sausage and cook until the meat is no longer red.
1 can (2 pounds) tomatoes 1 can (15 ounces) tomato sauce 1 can (12 ounces) tomato paste 1 teaspoon basil 1 teaspoon oregano 1 teaspoon sugar 2 tablespoons parsley salt and pepper	4. Mix in 1 can (2 pounds) tomatoes, 1 can (15 ounces) tomato sauce, 1 can (12 ounces) tomato paste, 1 teaspoon oregano, 1 teaspoon sugar and 2 tablespoons parsely.
	5. Let simmer 35-45 minutes stirring often. Salt and pepper to taste.
	6. Serve with grated Parmesan cheese over any kind of pasta.

Note: This is a basic recipe. Don't be afraid to experiment on your own gradually adding or subtracting ingredients according to your own taste preferences.

Notes:

Graham Cracker Crust

Difficlty rating: EASY

Equipment needed: 1 9½-inch pie plate, rolling pin & small saucepan

Serves: Yields 1 9½-inch crust

Estimated preparation time: 15-20 minutes

INGREDIENTS	BASIC STEPS
	1. Preheat oven at 350°.
28 graham crackers	2. With a rolling pin, crumble 28 graham crackers (about 2 cups).
½ cup butter or margarine	3. Melt ½ cup butter or margarine in a small saucepan.
¼ cup sugar	4. In a bowl, combine graham crackers with ¼ cup sugar and melted butter or margarine.
	5. Grease a pie plate with butter or margarine and press mixture against bottom and side with fingers or fork. Save leftover crumbs for topping.
	6. Bake for 15 minutes.

Notes:

Basic Pie Crust
(2 9½-inch crusts)

Difficulty rating: MODERATELY EASY

Equipment needed: Pastry blender (but can use a fork), pie plate & rolling pin

Serves: Yields 2 9½-inch crusts

Estimated preparation time: 15-20 minutes

INGREDIENTS	BASIC STEPS
ice cubes	1. Place some ice cubes in a small bowl of water.
2½ cups all-purpose flour 1 teaspoon salt	2. In a separate bowl, mix together 2½ cups all-purpose flour and 1 teaspoon salt.
1 cup shortening	3. Work in 1 cup shortening with a pastry blender or fork until mixture looks like fine crumbs.
7-8 tablespoons ice water	4. Sprinkle in ice water 1 tablespoon at a time up to 7-8 tablespoons mixing with a fork. When mixture is moistened, form into a ball with hands. Divide into two parts, one slightly larger than the other. Use bigger one for bottom crust.
	5. Place a slight amount of flour on a clean surface and flatten the dough out with a rolling pin until it is appropriate size for the pie plate (about 1/8 inch thick).
	6. Gently fit bottom crust in pie plate. Fill shell with desired filling and cover with top crust. Trim off overlap with knife. Press edges with the back prongs of a fork and cut 3-4 slits in top crust.

Notes:

Basic Pie Crust
(1 9½-inch crust)

Difficulty rating: MODERATELY EASY

Equipment needed: Pastry blender (but can use a fork), pie plate & rolling pin

Serves: Yields 1 9½-inch crust

Estimated preparation time: 15-20 minutes

INGREDIENTS

BASIC STEPS

1. Preheat oven at 450⁰.

ice cubes

2. Place some ice cubes in a small bowl of water.

1½ cups all-purpose flour
½ teaspoon salt

3. In a separate bowl, mix together 1½ cups all-purpose flour and ½ teaspoon salt.

½ cup shortening

4. Work in ½ cup shortening with a pastry blender or fork until mixture looks like fine crumbs.

4-5 tablespoons ice water

5. Sprinkle in ice water 1 tablespoon at a time up to 4-5 tablespoons, mixing with a fork. When mixture is moistened, form into a ball with hands.

6. Place a light amount of flour on a clear surface and flatten the dough out with a rolling pin until it is appropriate size for pie plate.

7. Gently fit crust in pie plate. Trim off overlap with knife. Press edges with the back prongs of a fork and prick holes in bottom and sides of shell.

8. Bake for 10-12 minutes.

Notes:

Hollandaise Sauce In A Blender

Difficulty rating: VERY EASY

Equipment needed: Blender & saucepan

Serves: Variable-makes about 1 cup

Estimated preparation time: 5-10 minutes

INGREDIENTS

¾ pound melted butter

4 egg yolks
2 tablespoons lemon juice
½ teaspoon salt
   dash of red pepper

BASIC STEPS

1. Melt ¾ pound of butter in a saucepan to the point of bubbling.

2. Combine in a blender, 4 egg yolks, 2 tablespoons lemon juice, ½ teaspoon salt and a dash of red pepper. Mix on high speed.

3. Turn blender to low speed and slowly add melted butter. Refrigerate what you don't use.

Notes:

French Dressing

Difficulty rating: VERY EASY

Equipment needed: Jar

Serves: Variable-makes about ⅓ cup

Estimated preparation time: 5-10 minutes

INGREDIENTS

¼ cup olive oil
1 tablespoon vinegar
1 tablespoon lemon juice
⅛ teaspoon paprika
¼ teaspoon dry mustard
¼ teaspoon sugar
salt and pepper

BASIC STEPS

1. In a jar, combine ¼ cup olive oil, 1 tablespoon vinegar, 1 tablespoon lemon juice, ⅛ teaspoon paprika, ¼ teaspoon dry mustard, ¼ teaspoon sugar and salt and pepper to taste.

2. Cover jar, shake well, and refrigerate. Shake again before using.

Notes:

Horseradish Sauce

Difficulty rating: VERY EASY

Equipment needed: Mixing bowl

Serves: Variable-makes about 1 cup

Estimated preparation time:
3-5 minutes

INGREDIENTS	BASIC STEPS
⅔ cup sour cream 2 tablespoons horseradish salt and pepper	1. In a bowl, combine ⅔ cup sour cream and 2 tablespoons horseradish. Salt and pepper to taste.

Notes:

Yogurt Dressing

Difficulty rating: VERY EASY

Equipment needed: Mixing bowl

Serves: Variable-makes about 1⅓ cups

Estimated preparation time: 5-10 minutes

INGREDIENTS

- 1 cup yogurt
- 3 tablespoons vegetable oil
- 1 tablespoon lemon juice
- 1 tablespoon curry powder

salt and pepper

BASIC STEPS

1. In a bowl, mix together 1 cup plain yogurt, 3 tablespoons vegetable oil, 1 tablespoon lemon juice, and 1 tablespoon curry powder.

2. Salt and pepper to taste and chill before serving.

Notes:

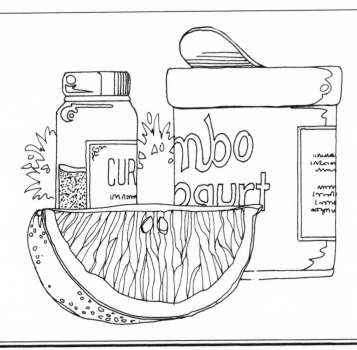

Blue Cheese Dressing

Difficulty rating: VERY EASY

Equipment needed: Mixing bowl

Serves: Variable-makes 2½ cups

Estimated preparation time:
5-10 minutes

INGREDIENTS

1 cup (4 ounces) blue cheese
1 package (3 ounces) cream cheese
⅔ cup mayonnaise
¼ cup milk or light cream
1 finely chopped clove of garlic
⅛ teaspoon paprika

BASIC STEPS

1. Combine in a bowl, 1 cup (about 4 ounces) blue cheese, 1 package (3 ounces) cream cheese, ⅔ cup mayonnaise, ¼ cup milk or light cream, 1 finely chopped clove of garlic and ⅛ teaspoon paprika.

2. Salt and pepper to taste and chill before serving.

salt and pepper

Notes:

Italian Dressing

Difficulty rating: VERY EASY

Equipment needed: Covered jar

Serves: Variable-makes about 1¼ cups

Estimated preparation time: 5-10 minutes

INGREDIENTS

 1 cup salad oil
⅓ cup vinegar
½ teaspoon salt
½ teaspoon onion salt
½ teaspoon oregano
½ teaspoon dry mustard
 1 garlic clove, finely chopped
    salt and pepper

BASIC STEPS

1. In a jar, combine 1 cup salad oil, ⅓ cup vinegar, ½ teaspoon salt, ½ teaspoon onion salt, ½ teaspoon oregano, ½ teaspoon dry mustard and 1 garlic clove, finely chopped. Salt and pepper to taste.

2. Cover jar, shake well and refrigerate. Shake again before using.

Notes:

Orange-Yogurt Syrup

Difficulty rating: VERY EASY

Equipment needed: Mixing bowl & grater

Serves: Makes 1½ cups

Estimated preparation time: 10-15 minutes

INGREDIENTS

- 1 cup plain yogurt
- ¼ cup orange juice
- ¼ cup sugar
- 1 teaspoon grated orange rind

BASIC STEPS

1. In a bowl, combine 1 cup plain yogurt, ¼ cup orange juice, ¼ cup sugar and 1 teaspoon grated orange rind. Mix thoroughly.

Notes:

Maple-Yogurt Syrup

Difficulty rating: VERY EASY

Equipment needed: Mixing bowl

Serves: Makes two cups

Estimated preparation time:
5-10 minutes

INGREDIENTS

1 cup plain yogurt
1 cup maple syrup

BASIC STEPS

1. In a bowl, combine 1 cup plain yogurt and 1 cup maple syrup. Mix thoroughly.

Notes:

Glossary of Terms
Used in This Book

Allspice — A spice that tastes like a combination of cinnamon, cloves, and nutmeg. Used in pickling, many dessert dishes, and on several meats. Can be purchased whole or ground in supermarkets.

All-purpose flour — As the name implies, this white flour is the most commonly used of all the flours for home baking. Can be purchased in supermarkets.

Anchovy — A small salt water fish of the herring family. Usually available tinned in salted, spiced oil. Can be purchased in supermarkets.

Antipasto — An Italian term referring to the appetizer course of a meal. It usually consists of cold hors d'oeuvres.

Bake — To cook something by dry heat in an oven.

Baking powder — A powdery substance consisting of several ingredients which is used to increase the size of dough. Can be purchased in supermarkets.

Barley — A grain used in soups and for making liquor. Can be purchased in supermarkets.

Baste — The process of moistening and/or flavoring meats while they are roasting by pouring the pan juices or special sauce over the surface.

Baster — A tube-like device with a large rubber bulb at the top. Used to suck up the liquids from a pan and redistribute them over the surface of the food being cooked.

Batter — A semiliquid mixture usually consisting of flour, water or milk, eggs and sugar, that can be easily stirred with a spoon.

Bay leaves — Aromatic green leaves used to flavor soups, stews, sauces and a variety of other dishes. Can be found in all supermarkets.

Bisque — A rich, creamy soup, the key component of which is shellfish.

Blend & blend in — The process of mixing a set of ingedients together until smooth and uniform.

Blue cheese — A term generally used to describe the blue-veined Roquefort-type cheeses. These crumbly-textured cheeses are especially good in salad dressings and as accompaniments to fruits. Can be purchased in supermarkets.

Bone — The process of removing the bone from fish, meats, or poultry.

Bouillon cube — A concentrated cube of clear chicken, beef or vegetable soup which can be reconstituted by adding hot water. Can be purchased in supermarkets.

Brewer's yeast — A by-product of brewing process. High in many of the B-vitamin group and an excellent source of protein. Can be purchased in health food stores.

Brie — A soft cheese encased in a white mold-like rind and produced in various sized wheels. Thus the term brie wheel. Can be purchased in supermarkets.

Broil — Cooking something by exposing it to direct heat. This is typically done through use of an oven broiler or barbecue.

Broth — Used interchangably with stock. The liquid that is left after cooking a food such as fish, poultry, meat, beans and so on.

Brown — The process of rendering foods brown by cooking them at higher heat either in an oven or on a top burner.

Brown sugar — This is sugar that has varying quantities of molasses; the darker the sugar the greater the concentration of molasses. Can be found in supermarkets.

Brush — The process of spreading melted butter, sauces, milk, and the like, over a solid food, usually with a pastry brush.

Buckwheat flour — Flour made from buckwheat kernels. Can be found in supermarkets and health food stores.

Canadian bacon — Made from boned pork loins. Canadian bacon has considerably less fat than American-style bacon which comes from the fatty sides and back of the pig. Can be found in supermarkets.

Cardamon — An Indian spice typically used to flavor desserts. Can be found in supermarkets.

Caviar — The roe or eggs of fish. Salty to the taste, it is generally used as an hors d'oeuvre. Can be found in supermarkets and in all gourmet food shops.

Chafing dish — A decorative serving dish that is used to cook and keep foods warm while presenting them attractively.

Cheddar — By far the most common of the American cheeses. Flavor ranges from mild to sharp. Especially good for cooking. Can be purchased in supermarkets.

Chill — To cool a substance throughout without freezing it.

Chili powder — A spice consisting of ground chili peppers and other spices. Used in flavoring chili and other Mexican-style dishes. Can be found in supermarkets.

Chop — The process of cutting food into smaller pieces. Usually done with a knife and chopping block, blender or food processor. The size of the pieces is designated by terms such as "finely chopped," "coarsely chopped," and so on.

Chowder — A milk-based stew or soup usually made from corn, clams, oysters or fish.

Cinnamon — A spice available in sticks or ground which is obtained from the bark of the cinnamon tree. Widely used in various types of cooking and baking. Can be found in supermarkets.

Clove — A single section of a larger bulb such as a "garlic clove." Also, a spice made from the buds of clove trees.

Coat — The process of completely covering the outer surface of a food with a substance such as bread crumbs, flour and the like.

Cointreau — An orange-flavored liqueur. Can be purchased in liquor stores.

Colander — A large bowl-shaped, sieve-like container used for draining foods.

Cool — To allow foods to return to room temperature.

Coriander — An herb, available as whole seeds or ground, that is used to flavor a variety of foods. Can be found in supermarkets.

Corn meal — A coarse meal made from yellow or white corn. Can be purchased in supermarkets.

Corn starch — Fine white flour made from corn. Used as a thickening agent. Can be found in supermarkets.

Cottage cheese — A soft, curd-like cheese made from skim milk. Can usually be substituted in recipes calling for Ricotta cheese. Can be found in supermarkets.

Cream cheese — A soft, mild, delicately flavored cheese. Has a wide variety of uses in cooking. Can be purchased in supermarkets.

Creme de cacao — A chocolate flavored liqueur made from the cocoa bean. Can be found in liquor stores.

Cream de menthe — A mint-flavored liqueur. Can be found in liquor stores.

Croutons — Small cubes of fried or toasted bread. Served with soups or salads as a garnish. Can be purchased in supermarkets.

Cube — To cut food into cubes ½ inch or larger.

Cumin — A spice, available as whole seeds or ground, that is used to flavor a variety of foods. Can be found in supermarkets.

Curry powder — A blend of spices including cumin, coriander, tumeric and ginger, which is a central ingredient in Indian cooking. Can be found in supermarkets.

Dice — To cut food into small cubes-usually less than ½ inch.

Dollop — A clump or blob, as of sour cream.

Dot — To sprinkle small pats, usually butter or margarine, over food.

Double boiler — A device consisting of two pans fitted together one on top of the other. The bottom one is filled with water and the top one contains whatever food one needs to cook or keep warm without direct heat.

Dough — A thick, flour-based mixture that is too stiff to stir or mix and must therefore be worked or kneaded with the hands.

Drain — The process of straining the liquid from the solid food, usually through the use of a sieve or colander.

Feta cheese — A Greek cheese with a semisoft, crumbly consistency. Can be purchased in supermarkets.

Fettuccine — An Italian word referring to noodles measuing approximately ¼ inch wide. Can be found in supermarkets.

Fillet — A piece of meat or fish that is without bone.

Flambe — French word meaning burned. In its general usage it refers to a dish that has a liquor poured over it and lighted with a match.

Florets — The smaller clusters making up the head or stalk of a vegetable such as cauliflower or broccoli.

Flounder — A mild-tasting fish with white flesh. Similar to sole. Can be purchased frozen or fresh in supermarkets.

Flour — See all-purpose, buckwheat, whole wheat and rye flour.

Fold in — The process of gently combining a set of ingredients with a large spoon or whisk so as to prevent the loss of air from light substances such as whipped cream or beaten egg whites.

Fontina cheese — An Italian cheese semisoft in texture. Can be purchased in supermarkets.

Frittata — An Italian word referring to a kind of omelet.

Garlic — A strong-flavored bulb consisting of smaller sub-units called cloves. Widely used in flavoring a variety of dishes. Can be found in supermarkets.

Garlic press — A device used to squeeze the juice from a garlic clove.

Garnish — A decorative, usually edible, addition to foods. Used to add flavor and/or aesthetic appeal to a dish.

Gazpacho — A Spanish word referring to a cold soup.

Ginger — A pungent-flavored root which can be purchased whole or ground. Used to flavor a variety of dishes. Can be found in supermarkets.

Grand Marnier — An orange-flavored liqueur. Can be purchased in liquor stores.

Grate — the process of rubbing food against a grater for the purpose of reducing it to tiny pieces.

Grater — A metal instrument covered with several types of rough surfaces. Used by cooks to manually shred or grate vegetables, cheeses and many other kinds of foods.

Grease — To cover the surface of a baking sheet, dish or pan with a thin layer of fat or oil to prevent sticking.

Griddle — A flat metal pan that is used for cooking french toast, pancakes and the like.

Grind — The process of reducing a food substance to tiny bits, usually through the use of a blender or food processor.

Herbs — Plants whose leaves or stems are used for seasoning other foods.

Hors d'oeuvres — Small appetizers which are served before the main course.

Horseradish — A strong-flavored root that is usually ground into a paste-like consistency with vinegar and salt and used as an accompaniment to meats or as an ingredient in various sauces. Can be purchased in root form or as a sauce in supermarkets.

Kettle — A big metal container used to cook soups, chili, pasta or any food that needs to be cooked in a large volume of liquid. Average sizes range from six to twelve quarts.

Knead — The process of working bread dough with the hands. Typically, this is done by rounding the dough into a ball and then pressing it down and away from the body with the heels of palms over and over again until dough is smooth and satiny.

Lecithin — Naturally occurring compounds similar to glycerides which are prepared commercially from soy beans and egg yolks. Can be purchased in granular or liquid form in health food stores and supermarkets.

Lime — The fruit of the lime tree. This green, tart-flavored fruit is used both as a garnish and to flavor a variety of dishes. Can be found in supermarkets.

Linguine — An Italian word referring to noodles measuring approximately 1/8 inch wide. Can be found in supermarkets.

Mace — A spice made from the fleshy outer husk of the nutmeg seed. Can be found in supermarkets.

Maraschino cherry — Very sweet, red cherries bottled in heavy syrup. Used in a variety of cocktails and as a garnish. Can be found in supermarkets.

Marinade — A mixture of liquids that is used to soak solid foods so as to flavor and/or tenderize them.

Marinate — The process of soaking a solid food in a liquid substance called a marinade.

Marjoram — An herb of the mint family which is used to flavor a wide variety of dishes. Can be found in supermarkets

Melba toast — Extremely thin, dry slices of bread which have been toasted until crisp. Can be found in supermarkets.

Melt — To reduce a solid food such as

209

butter to a liquid through the use of heat.

Mince — The process of reducing food to very tiny pieces through the use of a food processor, blender or knife.

Mint — An aromatic leaf which is used as a garnish and as an herb to flavor a wide variety of dishes. Can be purchased fresh or dried in supermarkets.

Mix — The process of combining a set of ingredients until a uniform consistency is reached.

Monterey Jack cheese — A semisoft American cheese which is excellent for melting. Can be found in supermarkets.

Mozzarella — A mild, semisoft cheese made from cows milk. A key ingredient in making pizza and eggplant or veal parmigiana. Can be found in supermarkets.

Oil — Usually referred to as vegetable oil, this is fat extracted from corn, peanuts, olives, soy beans and the like. Some products are a combination of more than one kind of oil.

Oregano — An herb closely akin to marjoram. Widely used in Italian cooking. Can be found in supermarkets.

Paprika — A seasoning, bright red in color, which is made from dried red pepper. Used as a garnish and to flavor a wide variety of foods. Can be purchased in supermarkets.

Pare — The process of removing the outer covering of fruits and vegetables with a knife or vegetable parer.

Parmesan — A hard, full flavored cheese which is usually grated to serve over a wide variety of dishes. Can be found in supermarkets either whole or grated.

Parsley — A green, leafy herb used as a garnish and to flavor a wide variety of foods. Can be purchased fresh or dried in supermarkets.

Pastrami — Cured, highly spiced smoked beef. Can be purchased precooked or uncooked in supermarkets.

Pastry blender — A utensil consisting of several wire loops connected to a handle. Used to cut shortening into flour in making pastry.

Pastry brush — A utensil that looks like a small paint brush. Used to spread melted butter and the like over breads and pastries.

Pate — A French word referring to any one of several seasoned meats which has been chopped or ground for use as a spread. Typically served as an appetizer. Can be purchased at supermarkets and gourmet food shops.

Peel — The outer rind or covering of selected fruits or vegetables. Also, the process of removing this covering.

Pepper, white or black — Black pepper is made from the entire berry or peppercorn of the pepper plant. White pepper, the milder of the two, is also ground from the peppercorn but with the outer husk removed. Can be purchased in supermarkets.

Peppercorn — The whole berry of the pepper plant. Used in pepper grinders for making freshly ground pepper. Can be purchased in supermarkets.

Pimiento — Sweet red peppers. Used as a garnish and in salads. Can be purchased is supermarkets.

Pinch — A term used to designate the amount of a substance that can be held between one's index finger and thumb. Less than ⅛ of a teaspoon.

Poach — To cook a food gently, just below the boiling point, in just enough water to cover it.

Powdered sugar — Also, called confectioners' sugar, this is an extremely fine grind of sugar that is powdery in appearance. Can be purchased in supermarkets.

Preheat oven — To heat an oven to a desired temperature before adding the food to be baked.

Prosciutto — An Italian word referring to paper thin slices of cured ham. Has a variety of uses in cooking. Can be found in supermarkets and in gourmet food shops.

Provolone cheese — An Italian cheese that is hard and cream colored. Can be puchased in supermarkets.

Puree — The process of turning food into a smooth paste through the use of a blender or food processor.

Rib — A single stalk detached from a larger bunch of celery.

Ricotta — Often referred to as the "Italian cottage cheese." Soft textured and moist, this cheese is used in a wide variety of dishes. Can be found in supermarkets.

Roast — The process of cooking something, usually meat, fish, poultry or game by dry heat in an oven.

Roaster — A large pan, covered or uncovered, especially designed for roasting meat.

Roll out — The process of rolling dough onto a flat surface with a rolling pin.

Romano — A hard, sharp Italian cheese. Can be grated to serve over various foods. Can be found in supermarkets.

Rosemary — A sweet tasting herb. Used to flavor a wide variety of dishes. Can be found in supermarkets.

Rye flour — Flour produced from rye grains. Can be purchased in supermarkets and health food stores.

Sage — An herb popularly used in poultry stuffing. Can be found in supermarkets.

Sake — Japanese wine made from fermented rice. Usually served warm. Can be purchased in most liquor stores.

Salami — A highly spiced sausage commonly used in sandwiches or salads. Can be found in supermarkets.

Saute — To cook food very gently in a skillet with a small amount of oil.

Scallions — Young green or spring onions. Can be found in supermarkets.

Scallops — The cube-shaped muscles of any of the several types of shellfish. Can be found in supermarkets and fish markets.

Score — The process of cutting shallow, lattice-like grooves in the outer surface of food.

Season — The process of adding seasonings to a set of ingredients.

Seed — The process of removing the seeds from fruit or vegetables.

Self-rising flour — All-purpose flour to which rising agents have been added. When using this type of flour, cooks must be careful to omit the baking powder and salt that is called for when all-purpose flour is used in a recipe.

Shallots — Small onion bulbs. Can be found in supermarkets.

Sherry — A sweet appetizer wine that is also widely used in cooking. Cooking sherry can be found in supermarkets.

Shortening — A generic term referring to the many kinds of solid fats used in cooking.

Shred — The process of transforming food into thread-like pieces through the use of a manual grater, blender or food processor.

Shuck — The process of removing the outer husk of corn. Also, removing the shell from shellfish such as oysters and clams.

Sieve — A screen-like device that is available in various bowl-shaped sizes. Used to drain liquids from solid foods.

Sift — The process of passing a set of dry ingredients, one of which is usually flour, through a sifter or sieve to remove coarse particles.

Simmer — The process of cooking foods in a liquid that is kept just below the boiling point.

Skillet — A frying pan. Comes in various sizes with or without covers.

Sliver — The process of cutting food into narrow, elongated strips. Commonly done with almonds.

Sole — A mild tasting fish with white flesh. Can be purchased in supermarkets.

Sour cream — Specially prepared sour cream that is used for a variety of cooking purposes. Can be purchased in supermarkets.

Soy sauce — A salty sauce used in Oriental cooking. Can be found in supermarkets.

Soya powder — A high protein flour produced from the seed of the soybean plant. Can be purchased in health food stores.

Spanish olives — Green olives which have been stuffed with a strip of pimiento pepper. Can be found in supermarkets.

Spatula — A wide, flat, blade-like instrument made of metal, wood, rubber or plastic that is used for spreading soft mixtures over various surfaces and/or for scraping the sides of bowls, dishes or pans.

Stew — The process of simmering food in a small amount of liquid over low to moderate heat in a covered pan. Also, the food so cooked.

Stir — The process of mixing a set of ingredients with a spoon in a round-and-round motion until the desired consistency is achieved.

Swiss cheese — A semi-hard cheese with a mild, nut-like flavor. Has a wide variety of uses in cooking. Can be purchased in supermarkets.

Tabasco — An extremely hot red pepper sauce. Can be found in supermarkets.

Taco — A crispy or soft tortilla into which a combination of ingredients is placed. Can be purchased in supermarkets.

Tarragon — An herb which is used to flavor a wide variety of dishes. Can be found in supermarkets.

Tartar sauce — A mayonnaise-based sauce that is commonly served with fish. Can be found in supermarkets.

Thyme — An herb which is used to flavor a wide variety of dishes. Can be found in supermarkets.

Turbot — A mild-tasting fish with white flesh. Can be purchased in supermarkets.

Tumeric — A finely ground spice that is a basic ingredient in curry powder. Can be found in supermarkets.

Vermouth — Sweet or dry appetizer wines. Dry vermouth is white in color while the sweet variety is darker in color. Can be found in liquor stores, wine shops and supermarkets.

Vichyssoise — A French word referring to a cold creamy potato soup.

Wheat germ — The inner or embryo portion of wheat grains. High in protein and selected B vitamins. Can be found in supermarkets.

Whip — The process of beating a food substance rapidly with a wisk or electric mixer so as to inflate it with air.

Whipping cream — Commonly referred to as heavy cream. Contains more than 30 perecent butter fat. Can be found in supermarkets.

Whisk — A utensil made of wire that is used to beat or whip foods such as eggs, creams and sauces.

Whole wheat flour — Flour made from the complete grain of wheat. Can be purchased in supermarkets and health food stores.

Yeast — Microscopic plants that "act" upon sugars to produce carbon dioxide. Used in baking and brewing. Can be purchased either compressed or dry in supermarkets.

Yogurt — A milk-based product that is slightly sour to the taste and creamy in texture. Used to flavor a wide variety of foods and eaten by itself. Can be found in supermarkets and health food stores.

Zucchini — A dark green Italian squash. Can be found in supermarkets.

Appendix A

*STOCKING AND EQUIPPING A KITCHEN

Following is a listing of the kitchen equipment needed to do the recipes in this beginner's guide. Also included here is the basic stockpile of foods that the average cook will want to have on hand for day-to-day cooking.

Before purchasing a single item on this chart, two bits of advice are in order. First, don't rush out and buy everything in one fell swoop. Rather, build up your basic kitchen supplies and equipment gradually in accordance with your evolving needs. Second, if you're interested in saving money, take a little time to shop the discount stores. The prices are much cheaper and, given the needs of most beginning cooks, the quality of the items is more than adequate. Accordingly, I have included the bottom range prices of the various products to help guide the careful shopper.

I. A STARTER SET OF KITCHEN TOOLS

ITEM	PRICE RANGE
Electrical Equipment	
Blender	$25.00 to 35.00
Sub-total for electrical equipment	$25.00 to 35.00
Assorted Pots, Pans, Skillets and Bowls	
2 Skillets; 1 six-inch and	$ 7.50 to 10.00
1 twelve-inch	$14.00 to 20.00
1 Griddle	$12.50 to 16.00
1 Tea Kettle (2½ quarts)	$ 8.50 to 15.00
2 Saucepans; 1 one-quart and	$ 7.00 to 10.00
1 three-quart	$10.00 to 15.00
1 Soup Kettle (six-quart)	$ 8.00 to 12.00
1 Roaster Pan (12"-15" long)	$ 4.50 to 8.00
1 Casserole Dish (two-quart)	$ 3.50 to 5.00
3 Mixing bowls (three-piece set)	$ 5.75 to 8.00
Sub-total for pots, pans, skillets, and bowls	$76.75 to 111.00

---

*This itemization not only makes an excellent shopping list for someone interested in outfitting his own kitchen, it can be profitably used by anyone who is looking for gift ideas for young marrieds, recent divorcees or friends and relatives who are about to move into their first apartment.

Baking Accessories

Item	Price Range
2 Pie Plates; 1 9", and	$ 2.75 to 3.00
1 9½"	$ 3.00 to 3.50
2 Loaf Pans (9" x 5")	$ 1.75 to 4.50
1 Twelve-cup Muffin Pan	$ 3.15 to 4.50
1 Baking Sheet (15¼" x 10¼" x ¾")	$ 3.50 to 4.50
1 Baking Dish (three-quart)	$ 6.50 to 8.50
1 Baking Dish (8" x 8" x 2")	$ 2.60 to 3.50
1 Baking Dish (9" x 9" x 2")	$ 3.00 to 4.00
1 Tube Pan (12 cup)	$ 6.75 to 9.00
1 Pizza Pan (12" x ½")	$ 2.00 to 5.00
Sub-total for baking accessories	$36.40 to 54.50

Basic Utensils

Item	Price Range
1 Hardwood Chopping Board	$ 6.00 to 10.00
1 Grater	$ 1.50 to 3.00
1 Egg Beater (manual)	$ 4.50 to 7.00
1 Colander	$ 3.50 to 5.00
1 Glass Measuring Cup (2-cup)	$ 2.85 to 4.00
1 Set Plastic Measuring Scoops/Spoons	$ 2.15 to 3.50
1 Vegetable Peeler	$ 1.35 to 2.00
1 Large Kitchen Spoon	$ 1.25 to 2.00
1 Large Cooking Fork	$ 1.25 to 2.00
1 Rubber Spatula	$ .89 to 1.50
1 Slotted Spoon	$ 1.00 to 3.00
1 Can Opener (manual)	$ 1.55 to 5.00
1 Pancake Turner	$ 1.25 to 3.00
1 Rolling Pin	$ 4.25 to 6.00
1 Potato Masher	$ 1.50 to 3.00
1 Set Wooden Spoons	$ .75 to 3.00
1 Funnel	$ .75 to 3.00
1 Melon Scoop	$ 1.50 to 3.00
1 Tongs	$ 1.00 to 2.00
1 Knife Sharpener (manual)	$ 2.40 to 5.00
3 Knives; 1 paring	$ 1.05 to 3.00
1 slicing	$ 4.00 to 7.00
1 chef's	$ 5.50 to 9.00
2 Pot Holders	$ 1.50 to 2.50
Sub-total for basic utensils	$55.74 to 98.50

GRAND TOTAL $193.89 to 299.00

Kitchen Equipment that is Nice But Not Necessary

Toaster	Juicer	Baster
Electric Mixer	Crepe Pan	Kitchen Scissors
Food Processor	Omelette Pan	Whisk
Electric Coffee Maker	Electric Can Opener	Garlic Press
Waffle Iron	Meat Thermometer	Electric Frying Pan
Dutch Oven	Scales	Bean Pot
Wok	Vegetable Steamer	Double Boiler

II. A Stockpile of Kitchen Staples

On The Spice Rack
Allspice
Basil
Bay Leaves
Cayenne Pepper
Celery Salt
Chili Powder
Cinnamon (ground)
Thyme

Cloves (whole or
    ground)
Curry Powder
Dill
Garlic Powder
Ginger (ground)
Lemon Salt
Marjoram

Mustard Powder
Nutmeg
Oregano
Paprika
Pepper
Rosemary
Salt
Sage
Tarragon

In The Cupboard
Sugar (white & brown)
Flour (all-purpose and
    whole wheat
Rice
Dried Navy Beans
Kidney Beans
Assorted Pasta
Bread Crumbs
Coffee
Tea

Catsup
Mustard
Pickles
Olives
Tabasco Sauce
Worcestershire Sauce
Vinegar
Vegetable Oil
Syrup

Jelly
Tuna Fish
Assorted Soups
Paper Towels
Aluminum Foil
Saran-type Wrap
Plastic Bags
Dish Soap
Scratch Pads
Sponge

In The Refrigerator
Mayonnaise
Milk
Cheese
Onions
Potatoes
Bacon
Assorted Salad Dressings
Assorted Fruits

Garlic
Assorted Frozen Vegetables
Eggs
Butter or Margarine
Lettuce
Bread
Parmesan Cheese

Appendix B

PUTTING IT ALL TOGETHER:
MENU SUGGESTIONS WITH MEN IN MIND*

Breakfasts

CONTINENTAL BREAKFAST

Orange Juice or Curried Tomato
Juice
Corn Muffins
Blueberry Muffins
Assorted Jellies
Coffee or Tea

COUNTRY BREAKFAST

Grapefruit Juice
Cottage Cheese Scramble
Bacon or Ham
Home Fried Potatoes
Toast & Jelly
Coffee or Tea

BREAKFAST FOR WEEKEND
GUESTS

Fruit Salad
Onion and Pepper Frittata
Toast & Jelly
Coffee or Tea

AN ELEGANT BREAKFAST FOR
TWO

Champagne
Fresh Raspberries or Strawberries
in Cream
Eggs Benedict
Coffee or Tea

Brunch/Lunch Menus

LUNCH WITH THE KIDS

English Muffin Pizza
Banana Cream Pie
Milk

LUNCH FOR COMPANY

Gazpacho
Bread Sticks
Broiled Open-Faced Cheese & Olive
Sandwich
Assorted Pickles
Peaches in Sour Cream
Choice of Wines
Coffee or Tea

SUPER SUNDAY SPREAD

An Assortment of Your Guests'
Favorite Drinks
Party Cheese Ball
Assorted Crackers
Chili with Wine
Cold Sandwich Platter
Assorted Breads
Potato Chips and Pretzels
Pickles, Olives & Condiments
Blueberry Cake
Coffee or Tea

A BEFORE THE GAME BRUNCH

Bloody Marys
Cheddar Cheese Soup
Cold Sandwich Platter
Assorted Breads
Olives, Pickles & Condiments
Quick Coffee Cake
Coffee or Tea

AN ITALIAN BRUNCH

Antipasto
Linguine with Clam Sauce
Garlic Bread
Chianti and/or Soave Wine
Spumoni Ice Cream
Anisette Liqueur
Coffee

*All menus are comprised of recipes presented in this book.

A LUNCH TO LINGER OVER

Champagne
Cream Cheese & Caviar
Gingered Lamb Chops
Asparagus Hollandaise
Home Made Muffins
Chocolate-Brandy Dessert
Coffee or Tea

Dinner Menus

NICE N' EASY DINNER FOR COM-PANY

Prosciutto and Melon
Bread Sticks
Fettuccine Alfredo
Tossed Salad
Choice of Dressings
Warm Bread
Ice Cream Grasshopper Dessert
Choice of Wines
Coffee or Tea

NICE N' EASY DINNER FOR COM-PANY

Grilled Oysters and Bacon Appetizers
Cornish Hen with Walnut Stuffing
Orange Glazed Beets
Muffins
Banana-Coffee Dessert
Choice of Wines
Coffee or Tea

HURRY UP DINNER

Broiled Fish Fillets with Curry
Grilled Tomatoes
Bread
Your Favorite Ice Cream
Coffee or Tea

HURRY UP DINNER

Linguine with Clam Sauce
Tossed Salad
Bread
Your Favorite Sherbet
Coffee or Tea

HURRY UP DINNER

Pork Chops with Plum Sauce
Tossed Salad
Bread
Peaches in Sour Cream
Coffee or Tea

DOLLAR STRETCHING DINNER

Cheese-Zucchini Casserole
Bread or Muffins
Coffee or Tea

DOLLAR STRETCHING DINNER

Tortilla Bake
Bread or Muffins
Coffee or Tea

DOLLAR STRETCHING DINNER

Italian Casserole
Tossed Salad
Garlic Bread
Coffee or Tea

INTIMATE DINNER FOR TWO

Choice of Appetizer Wines
Cream Cheese and Caviar
French Style Veal
Asparagus Hollandaise
Bread
Choice of Dinner Wines
Chocolate-Brandy Dessert
Choice of Dessert Wines
Coffee or Tea

A FIRESIDE APPETIZER DINNER FOR TWO

Choice of Wines
Stuffed Figs
Cheese Spread
Chicken Liver Pate
Broiled Scallops Wrapped in Bacon
Assorted Crackers & Breads
Ice Cream Grasshopper Dessert
Coffee or Tea

Appendix C

CONVERSION CHART FOR OVEN TEMPERATURES

Fahrenheit Degrees	Heat Descriptor	Centigrade Degrees
200-225	Warm	93-107
250-275	Very Low	121-135
300-325	Low	149-163
350-375	Medium	177-191
400-425	High	204-218
450-475	Very High	232-246
500-525	Extremely High	260-274
600	Broil	316

Basic formula for converting Fahrenheit temperatures to Centigrade:
1. Begin with Fahrenheit temperature,
2. subtract 32,
3. multiply by 5,
4. divide by 9, and the result equals Centigrade temperature equivalent.

Basic formula for converting Centigrade temperatures to Fahrenheit:
1. Begin with Centigrade temperature,
2. multiply by 9,
3. divide by 5,
4. add 32 and result equals Fahrenheit temperature eqluivalent.

Conversion Tables For Standard Weights And Measures

Common Units of Weight

1 ounce = 28.35 grams	1 gram = .035 ounces
16 ounces = 1 pound	1000 grams = 1 kilogram
1 pound = 453.59 grams	1 kilogram = 2.21 pounds

Common Units of Volume

Unit	U.S. Equivalent	Metric Equivalent*	Metric Cup Equivalent*
1 teaspoon	60 drops	5 milliliters	5 milliliters
1 tablespoon	3 teaspoons	15 milliliters	15 milliliters
1 ounce	2 tablespoons	30 milliliters	30 milliliters
¼ cup	4 tablespoons	59 milliliters	60 milliliters
⅓ cup	5⅓ tablespoons	79 milliliters	80 milliliters
½ cup	8 tablespoons	118 milliliters	125 milliliters
1 cup	16 tablespoons	237 milliliters	250 milliliters
2 cups	1 pint	473 milliliters	500 milliliters
2 pints	1 quart	1 liter (about)	

*Metric recipes are based on metric cup measurements which are inflated slightly to simplify conversion.

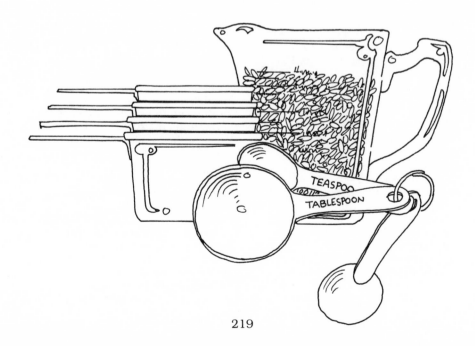

219

Index